SECTION ONE

SYSTEMS

Andreas Sofroniou

CONTENTS: PAGE:

INFORMATION SYSTEMS

There can be little doubt that Information System, the Internet, and Information Technology in general, is, and will be increasingly important in the years ahead.

This book has been designed for the business person, for the student and the systems professional who needs an overview regarding the logical analysis in Information Technology and the systems involved. The book explores the fundamental aspects of operational computing, the development of new information systems, and the structured methodologies used. Systems Analysis is discussed according to their structure and the book focuses on further developments in information technology and their planning.

In writing the book, the author is mostly concerned with the logical analysis and the managing of systems and people in multi-national corporations, software houses, government departments, the European Union, and academia.

In the past, the majority of data processing has been carried out by companies using batch style computer systems. With the cost of hardware rapidly reducing and with the hardware power and facilities increasing inversely, on-line and Internet systems are now becoming easier to justify and develop.

The objective of I.T. systems is to capture data, process it, and present the information. Because of the widespread use of the Internet, and all the versions of computers within business, it is sometimes assumed that data always refers to some type of financially oriented transaction. In fact, data has a more general meaning. In general terms, data can be used to denote any or all facts, numbers, letters, and symbols that refer to, or describe an object, idea, condition, or any other function. But data can only be of value if it can be organised in some way, so that it becomes meaningful to somebody; this is information.

The data must be checked for integrity, to ensure that errors have not arisen during any data capture processes. Data are compared to establish relationships, similarities, and differences. By now the data should have been completely processed, but to be proper information the processing results must be presented in such a way that it has relevance and meaning. Finally, the information must be produced on a medium that is legible.

In years bygone, on-line systems of any form have been difficult to justify because of the cost of:

- Additional hardware needed to sustain speedy response times,
- Systems software needed to support individual terminal activity,
- Additional design overhead for systems assurance.

With hardware power increasing and their costs reducing rapidly, these objectives are now disappearing.

Indeed, the justification for modern applications must be much easier now, when their benefits include:

- Speedier data entry,
- Reduced data error rates,
- Faster processing cycles,
- Quick response to user enquiries.

SYSTEMS PROBLEMS

Of all the major problems encountered in computing, the most difficult is the management of the systems and their development. Unlike any engineering or architectural drawings, the systems cannot be visibly represented as a model. Any building or machine can be shown as a set of drawings and as a three dimensional model, but the design and the build of the system cannot be seen, nor can it be represented on top of a desk.

In the case of an architectural concept, the designer will draw the plans and will supervise and delegate the tasks to builders to construct in a fashion, as close to perfect logistics as possible.

In modern computing, structured methodologies are used, where dataflow diagrams can be drawn, data can be modelled, and at the end of the logical phase, the system can be prototyped and programmed.

This brings forward the problem of managing, delegating, and guiding those who analyse the business requirements and the data on which the information is based; the professionals who proceed with the design based on the requirements and those who program and implement the required system.

In most cases, these activities are under one roof. Mainly, three different professions passing details to each other at the end of each developmental stage: Analysis, Designing, and Programming. The Information Technology Manager will need to know what each step of development involves and at every phase what the professional system engineer is doing. As in every other project, tasks need to be based on timescales and the financial implication to remain close to the budgets.

In commercial computing the financial costs for developing a new system are in six figures and in many cases where additional hardware and software are to be acquired, one project can be in the region of millions of pounds. To cope with such enormities of resources and the correct availability of business information, an organisation relies completely on the professional knowledge of its system analysts and those who manage the projects.

The media frequently report failures of systems and frustrations in computers at large. More often within companies, disappointments in systems are such that the computer department is totally isolated from other business activities. Yet, there are those companies whose total running of their business is based on the smooth running of their computer systems; the profitability and the revenue always ahead of their competitors.

But, it is also true to say that with all modern computing and devices, industry still suffers, or outputs could be improved, if only the computer department could design and operate a system the way the users work and based on the company's requirements.

The systems person is aware of these problems and yet cannot stretch his/her know-how any more than is already done. Imagine the various professionals under one roof, the complexity of designing and constructing systems, of the housekeeping involved, of the running and maintenance of all these sections.

If an organisation has many departments to enable it to function, so does the computer environment. In a superimposed mode, the Information Technology Manager has just as many sections to look after, admittedly on a smaller scale, but just as complex. Humans, machines, finances, stresses, productions, outputs, man-machine relationships, all in one department, just as much as any overall organisation is facing.

The I.T. Manager relies on management skills, systems knowledge, and various other business methods in order to give a good service to everybody in the company. The subject covers business computing and its management, the development of new systems, the implementation, and their running. The Manager in computing is aware of actual examples and will draw on projects and experience gained in building large and moderate systems based on what the users require, their problems, the solutions and their training in ensuring the success of the new system, or additional information technology modules.

In the first place, the expertise of those involved must cover the last generation of computing (which systems are still operating in many international organisations), its successes and its failures and the running in company environments. This includes the mainframe-based systems, the advent of PCs (Personal Computers) and their impact on networking and distributed processing, expert systems, shells, and artificial intelligence.

These, inevitably will be supported by training and experience in Structured Methodologies, a comparative study into methods, the use of the predominant systems architectures and a method for 'Rapid Building' system engineering.

Modern systems analysis, concentrates on the training aspect, the psychology of users, motivation and delegating specific to the computer departments, the interviewing techniques in gathering the information on current systems, the cataloguing of the problems and requirements, the appropriate solutions and their incorporation into the design of the required system.

Regarding the newcomers to the commercial computing professions, organisations rely on aspiring young graduates. With all good will they bring with them and with all their ambitions for the yuppie incomes, graduates still need the specialised training in computing and systems applications to business requirements.

It must be said that academia has progressed enormously in computing during the last ten years, but business needs differ from that of university research and studies. Graduates who enter the companies' surroundings find that they are unprepared for the demand of creating and using commercial systems in large organisations.

The early electronic computers of the 1940s had central processing units built up of banks of vacuum tubes, 'the glass bottles', also found in old wireless sets and television receivers. The CPUs (Central Processing Units), needed thousands of these tubes. The systems were cumbersome and unreliable, only hours between failures. There were heavy electrical power demands and the cooling plant was often as large as the computer.

The first computer of this type was ENIAC (Electronic Numerical Integrator and Computer), developed in the USA by J P Eckert and JW Mauchmy. ENIAC completed by 1946 was designed with the purpose of generating artillery firing tables. Built up of 18,000 vacuum tubes; it was immense, requiring a room 60 feet by 25 feet to hold it and weighing more than 30 tons.

In 1948, a transistor was first demonstrated by William Shockley, John Bardeen, and Walter Brattain, working in the Bell Telephone Laboratory, in the USA. Transistors could do virtually all the jobs of the then conventional vacuum tube valves, but required much less electrical power, generated very little heat and were much smaller. They were considerably more reliable and made possible the development of computers as effective functional devices in an increasingly wide range of applications.

The computers of the fifties and early sixties, individually used thousands of transistors. The various electronic components, transistors, resistors, capacitors, and diodes were mounted on printed circuit cards or boards. Copper was selectively edged from phenolic or fibreglass base to leave electrical connections between holes in which the wires of the components were inserted. A typical five-inch square printed circuit card would contain about a dozen transistors and a hundred or so other components.

Each computer (now second generation) comprised several thousand printed circuit cards. The cards, regarded as modules, were slotted into frames and interconnected by means of back-wiring. A typical large computer would be built up from several dozen specific modules, each of them being used up to several times in each computer.

In the sixties, the semi-conductor makers created a whole new technology, making possible the development of third generation computers. Using a more sophisticated version of transistor fabrication technology, it was possible to manufacture dozens of transistors together on a single small silicon chip. In this way an electronic circuit previously comprising many separate inter-connected components, could be manufactured as a single integrated unit.

By the early seventies, the basic components, transistors, diodes, etc. were assembled in a ten micro-millimetre thick surface layer in a silicon wafer. The components were then connected by metal layer evaporated on to the silicon. Subsequent etching produced a required inter-connection. Several of the integrated circuits could be mounted on a printed circuit card which could carry all the circuitry necessary for a central processing unit and the associated computer elements.

In recent years, integrated circuits were manufactured with a complexity of around one thousand transistors. The first micro-processor, produced by Intel Corporation in 1971, was based on a single quarter of an inch silicon chip which carried the equivalent of 2,250 transistors, all the necessary CPU circuitry for a tiny computer. By 1976, chips of this size using LSI (Large Scale Integration) could carry more than 20,000 components. Looking into the early part of the next millennium, the chip fabrication will allow larger chips to be built using smaller technology.

When a computer CPU is one integrated circuit, or a small number of circuits, the CPU is called a micro-processor. A micro-processor used with other integrated components forms a micro-computer.

With the introduction of Intel's Pentium and subsequent ranges, and other manufacturers' equivalent PC-based capacity and speed, together with the personal computers software such as the Microsoft hold users in amazement and difficulty in following the development in computing.

In general, all modern computers, Personal Computers (PCs), laptops, notebooks, i-pads, mobile telephones, etc. have similar architecture features, functional elements equivalent to those of an old and recent large mainframe. The PCs may vary in performance according to their storage capacity. However, these are encroaching on many application areas, formerly the exclusive province of the larger computers.

The cost of computer hardware is expected to fall even more with the development of new hardware and software in the next five years and it is expected that the resident operating languages and software will be given free as part of the hardware. Application software, in a packaged form and helpful in running commercial systems, will be of minimal cost.

Today, computing is affecting work and leisure alike, increasingly involved in factory and business operations, networking (social and otherwise), defence, medicine, education, and the domestic environment. They are influencing attitudes to privacy, employment and other social issues.

SYSTEMS ANALYSIS

The reader must remember that the construction of a system is as complex as a house built in a swamp. It requires careful planning and design. Just as a house must have an architect's plan, so does a system. It must have requirements, system objectives, and a blueprint; the Diagrammatic Representation of Systems

In general, it must be well noticed that every system structured is an answer to the users' problems and requirements. The solutions will be based on the studies of the current systems (manual and computerised), and the problems and requirements catalogue.

The design of the system will be based on how the users work and what suits the overall business environment. Whilst analysing the users' needs, the system analyst will proceed with the logical stages, by listening, interviewing, and having walkthroughs and reviews with users and colleagues.

Prior to proceeding into the physical stages development, the system analysts, designers and managers involved, will seek approval from the appropriate groups of people. Within the physical stages and during the construction of the system, the system builders will test and make the necessary alterations to the modules being implemented.

The users' systems acceptance will include all the necessary documentation and all the training and support required to ensure that the new system or module is successful.

The illustration of the generalised overall computing environment, (on the following page) can help in unravelling these complexities. The hierarchical diagram represents computing in large organisations. Within IT five major modules are included in a structured mode. Every module is diagrammatically represented, at different levels.

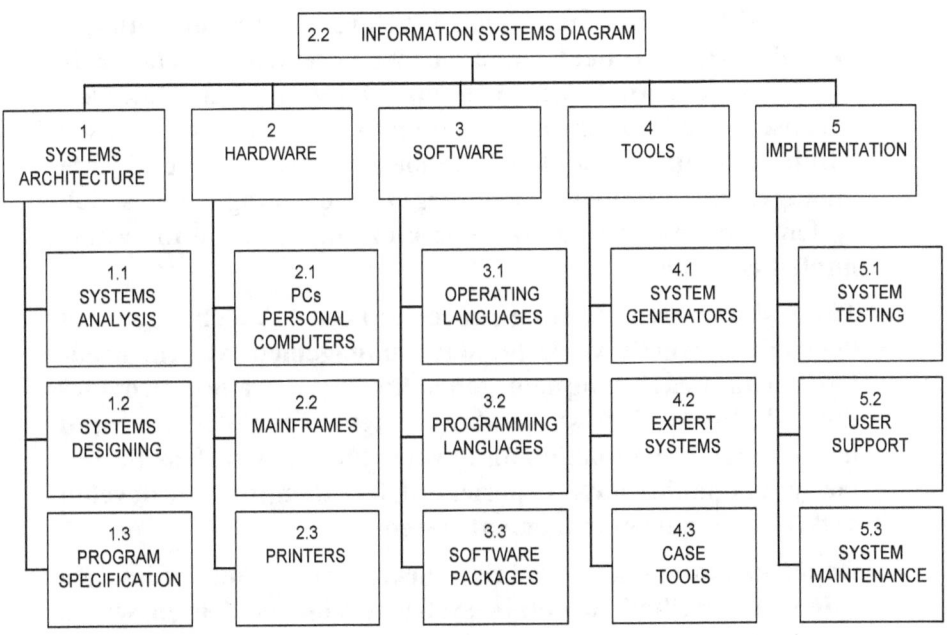

SYSTEMS ARCHITECTURE

The background of structured analysis and designing as an information engineering methodology, a technique-driven approach, started in 1972. Between 1980 and 1982, Gane and Sarson and Yourdon methodologies were extensively used. In 1983, business started using the information engineering automated version. By 1989, the information engineering development paths underwent further evolution. In 1992, the business re-engineering and object-oriented versions were introduced.

The need to control and manage the ever-increasing amounts of all organisational data being created, particularly computer-generated data, has gained recognition. However, because data management automates the processes used within a company, implementation is not easy. Several data management suppliers have begun requesting that a full systems and business analysis is undertaken prior to system implementation.

These show where existing processes need to be changed and determines exactly what the data management system needs to do within each unique organisation. It, therefore, provides the platform for successful systems architecture and management introduction and avoids the many pitfalls that so many companies have experienced in attempting to develop and install a new management system.

Rapid prototyping is gaining acceptance. Companies are using this method to obtain system design models in weeks rather than months, dramatically reducing lead-times and enabling better decisions and choice of system modules to be made.

A Systems Analyst in his/her approach defines the whole project, modularises it into manageable sections and proceeds in a logical manner according to the clear principles of user involvement.

The tasks are always broken down into structured, goal-oriented, meaningful units of work. The end result of these structured sets of tasks is applicable to the development path of:

- Information Strategy Planning,
- Business Area Analysis,
- Business Design/Technical Design,
- Construction,
- Transition,
- Production.

The above stages can be used by Analysts, Designers, Project Managers, Directors and Trainers in information technology methods to suit the technical and the user environment.

New techniques have been introduced that dramatically reduce the time taken to solve business and system problems. The result is that it is now possible to take the requirements, analyse, and view the results in days or weeks, rather than months. This, of course, makes analysis possible and cost-effective within the design process, rather than a special system task.

Recent years have seen further development in business and systems analysis software. Product releases of leading software houses have not only made systems architecture easier for everyday system engineers, but faster too. Closer links to CASE (Computer-aided Software Engineering) systems have made analysis simpler, while new interfaces make analysis understandable to users.

The term systems analysis is used in many computer installations in different ways. In fact, for most development projects it means the following:

- Fact finding,
- Operational analysis,
- Business system design.

System analysis for an organisation means that the analyst has more detailed work to do by establishing with the users that there is a justification for developing a new system.

Designing Systems

The interface between the user and a computer system has always been an important design factor. In interactive computer systems the interface (the dialogue) can influence not only the system's efficiency, but also its acceptability to the user.

The significance of effective dialogue design has its advantages and disadvantages:

- Computer initiated dialogues are initially effective for the novice user, but quickly fall into disfavour when the user becomes more familiar with the system,

- Equally, touch screen icons and 'short-hand' user initiated dialogues can only be used effectively by an experienced user.

Therefore, the first aspect of interface design is to determine who will be using the system and how frequently they will be using it.

It may be necessary to have two sets of dialogues for the same system. One for the trainees, icon users, and a 'short-hand' version for experienced staff.

The user psychology here is extremely important. The interface between the user and the system must be an extension of the way the user does his/her work. Any dialogue which causes deviation from this, will cause frustration and ultimately dislike for the system.

The second aspect of dialogue design is to ensure that the system is friendly and responsive.

Friendly means that:

- Screen formats are easy to read, data entry areas are clearly identified and error conditions are highlighted,
- Computer-displayed messages on the screens give the status of user initiated functions.

Responsive means that the computer should react to a user's request within a given response time, which is normally a low number of seconds.

In summary, the design of the system is significant because:

- It affects the character of the overall systems design,
- It directly affects user acceptability,
- Once committed to a design it is expensive to change.

The new technology is introducing techniques which are changing the way organisations work, as opposed to just addressing existing tasks. To successfully implement and apply the systems tools requires extensive education and it is this that is currently presenting the biggest hurdles for companies.

Computer security has become a challenge dominated by the improvements to information technology. Techniques are being developed to make access to systems harder. In recent years, much work has been done to make the computer recognise individual characteristics, unique to the user, such as eye contact, a signature, fingerprinting, or even the genetic print of DNA.

With users and companies becoming more dependent upon computer systems, the privacy and reliability of such systems are becoming critical aspects of design. Systems Assurance, a term which is currently popular, of a system embraces the parts of systems design which reduce the risk of both the fraudulent use of the system and lengthy recovery times in the event of a system's failure.

In many companies, one of the few problems that have to be resolved quickly is:

- Privacy,

- Fraudulent entry of data,

- Policing, a system must do more than just reporting violation,

- Effective restricted access at varying levels to different users,

- Recording access violations.

Users and companies are becoming more and more dependent upon resilience of computer-based systems. Computer systems can fail for a number of reasons.

Failures due to:

- Telecommunications,

- Hardware,

- Software,

- Networking.

Whichever the cause of the failure, the user will expect that the system can be recovered quickly and that the applications are free from data corruption.

Inconsistencies within applications can result in:

- Users losing confidence in the system,
- Lengthy investigation into the cause of failure,
- Protected systems down time whilst the data sets are reconstructed from source documentation.

Therefore, one significant aspect of recovery is the time taken to reconstruct application data sets. The most straightforward method of recovering is to duplicate them by backup. The advantage of a backup is that recovery after failure is extremely fast.

In various sensitive applications, frequent auditing is recommended. As a minimum, a daily control report should be produced, reconciling balances on the opening and closing versions of data sets. This report should also show in detail the origins of all transactions processed during the reporting period.

With the number of computer applications continuing to grow and with a similar increase in the number of people using them, a new type of back-up service is needed. To meet the demand, a number of companies have introduced guides to their applications, which include various types of catalogues. The catalogue, in fact, serves as a comprehensive system engineering tool.

Details on system applications, specifications, and service requirements are made available to all users. If a user is not sure what documents are needed, he/she can start by looking at the full index.

Companies are even making available dedicated internal e-mail messages and Internet pages, the latter being interactive and intelligent. Newsletters are published, which keep the users informed of new product developments, interesting applications, and other IT activities.

The widespread use of computers throughout business and the rapid growth of Internet connectivity mean that computer security should concern all organisations.

One simple measure to prevent unauthorised outsiders dialling into the system is to install dial-back modems. However, this security measure is easy to side-step. Likewise, calling-line identification, which permits the computer to identify the calling number and refuse access if it is not recognised, can be bypassed by the experienced people.

Encryption is essential for the transmission of any material passing down the line, broadband, and wi-fi. A simple method is to employ software which uses the same code at either end to encode and decode data. The next level is to impose a code of the day, using an encryption device card which is synchronised with a similar calculator card within the network.

The most complex form of encryption available is the digital signature. Each user has a private key linked to a public key made available on an electronic notice board. The user encodes the message with the private key and the message can be decoded by anyone holding the allocated public key. However, any message encoded with the public key can be decoded only by the holder of the private key.

SOFTWARE CONSIDERATIONS

Developing large systems require a range of software to achieve the overall objective. Depending upon the application and hardware types, this range of software at best could be totally packaged, or at worst may need to be completely written specially for the system.

Software in a project is like a jigsaw puzzle. Each piece fulfils a role and each piece must integrate with other pieces to make the complete system.

The basic types of software used are:

- Applications software,
- Conversational software,
- Database management software,
- System development software,
- Network software,
- System support software.

Applying hardware and software knowledge to system designing and the development of systems enables System Architects to choose individual applications from a range of developers and bring these together into a single system that best meets the needs of the company and its tasks, transparently, sharing data. It also enables standard software, such as spreadsheets, word-processing, presentation packages, and databases, to be linked to engineering software.

The flexibility this gives is far better for users than the traditional closed systems environment that forms the basis of many computing software packages. However, to take advantage of this environment the system developers must totally restructure their approach to system building, a complex, and daunting task.

As a background to structured methodology, it is worth mentioning that it all started with IBM and the problems this giant of computing was facing with the programming problems. IBM called in psychologist Larry Constantine who, as the story goes, diagnosed that the programmers were projecting their own individual perceptions of how the specifications were written.

Larry Constantine's write-up on a structured method included ideas from his psycho-physiological studies and terms such as afferent and efferent. His suggestions worked for IBM and soon after, others followed with variations. Names such as Gane and Sarson, Yourdon, James Martin, and other gurus, who again were followed by BIS Modus, LBMS-LSDM and with CCTA-SSADM and many, many more familiar names.

The differences among the protagonists were not of any consequence. Gane and Sarson used to say that all details could be gathered within a diagram and then modularise into smaller sections within boundaries. Yourdon maintained that anything bigger than an A4 paper was too complicated. Now-a-days, everybody is recommending five boxes on an average within a boundary, maximum seven and three the minimum. Any more than seven boxes and the analyst will take into consideration the possibility of decomposing to a lower level.

The point is that, instead of just picking up the keyboard of the dummy terminal and starting to program, everybody in the commercial world is now following a structured method. Whether the systems designed are successful or not, depends on the training and experience the systems engineers bear with them. In a similar way this is what the contents of this book are trying to assimilate.

NEED FOR STRUCTURED ANALYSIS

Systems Analysis consists of an evolving set of tools and techniques which have grown out of the success of structured designing. The underlying concept is the building of a logical model, a non-physical system, using a diagrammatic representation which enables the users and analysts to get a clear and common understanding of the required system. How its parts fit together and how it answers to the users' needs.

Since Computer-aided Software Engineering (CASE) tools are used to build a logical model, structured methodology involves building a system by successive refinement by:

- Producing an overall system dataflow diagram (DFD),
- Developing detailed dataflows,
- Defining the detail of data structure and process logic,

The whole of the analysis and designing of the system is done by employing a top-down method for:

- Analysing,
- Designing,
- Developing,
- Testing.

It is recognised that good development involves iteration, and an Analyst has to be prepared to refine the logical model and the physical design in the light of information resulting from the use of an early version of that model, or design. This may involve some reverse engineering of the processes of an earlier physical system, or an earlier version of the analysis exercise.

In many ways, systems analysis and designing is the toughest part of the development of an information technology system.

The problems encountered by an Analyst in a company environment will include:

- **Technical difficulty of the work,**
- Demand of knowledge of current technology,
- Political difficulties that arise,
- Several conflicting interest user groups,
- Communication difficulties among people of different backgrounds,
- Different views, requirements and priorities.

It is the compounding of these difficulties that makes systems analysis so demanding. It is a fact that the analyst becomes the middleman between user groups and has the intuitive approach for the users' problems and their solutions. The analyst must bring forward what is currently possible in an onrushing technology and what is optimum for the business run by people - making the match in a way which is acceptable to all.

Even with the best CASE tool, no methodology will enable the analyst to know what is in a user's mind and has no way of showing a tangible model of the system, apart from the diagrams of the logical phases and their short descriptions. On the other hand, it is hard for the users to imagine what the new system is going to do for them, until it is actually up and running, by which time it may be too late to perform any costly post-implementation repairs and additions.

To begin with, in order to ease the communication with the users, an analyst can use the tools of structured systems analysis to prepare a functional specification which:

- Is comprehended and agreed by the users,
- Sets out the logical requirements of the system without dictating a physical implementation,
- Expresses preferences and trade-offs.

The building of a logical model which clearly communicates to users what the systems will and will not do is crucially important. The users cannot afford to wait until the system is operational, before they see what they get. The analysing and designing of the logical phases are, therefore, of paramount importance in telling the users what to expect.

TOOLS FOR ANALYSIS

At a general level, it can be said that just like an existing system, the new system will represent (for example) the processing of orders from customers, the orders will be checked against a file of products available, check on a file holding a customer's details and then dispatch the goods with an invoice.

This can be shown in a logical data flow diagram (DFD):

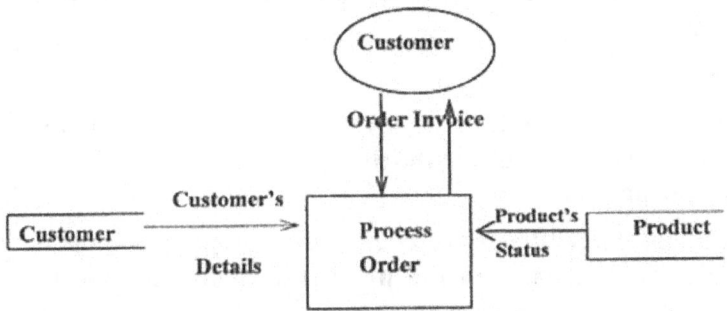

In this DFD four symbols were used:

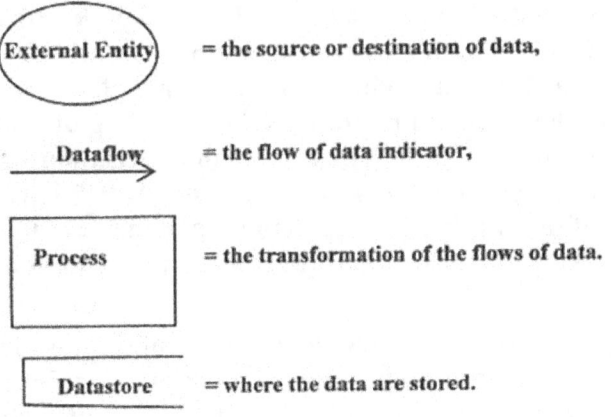

The symbols above and the concepts they represent, are at a logical level:

- An external entity may represent a client/customer, or another entity/department from within an organisation.

- A flow of data may physically be contained in a letter, or an invoice; anywhere data pass from one entity or process to another.

- A process may physically be a clerk calculating charges, or a combination of manual and automated activities.

- A datastore can be a card file, a filing cabinet, or a file on a tape or disk.

Using the four symbols enables the Analyst to draw a diagram of the system without committing the system as to how it will be implemented.

The example of 'Process Order' can be expanded to show the logical functions within the present system. The checking of incoming orders can be shown. Once the orders have been validated, a supplier can be found who is willing to give discounts on large orders.

The DFD (data flow diagram) that follows shows the checking of each order and in return the assembling of bulk orders to the supplier, to benefit from a discount. In this DFD a boundary has been introduced to separate the external entities from the activities relating to the 'handling of orders'. In a way the boundary signifies the modularisation of the processes in the functions relating to 'verifying and assembling of orders' (within the 'handling'), the data flowing to and from various 'boxes' and the storing of the data in the datastores.

The example shown is of course a summary of a lot of details regarding orders. Normally, the average of five boxes is shown within a boundary and further details are always shown in the exploded, lower level of the DFD. If necessary,

each component process box can itself be broken down to a third level of detail.

Within the boundaries of the top level and the subsequent exploded second and third levels, other processes will be introduced. In elaborating the example of 'orders', processes such as 'invoicing', 'accounts receivable', 'assign shipment' etc. will be introduced.

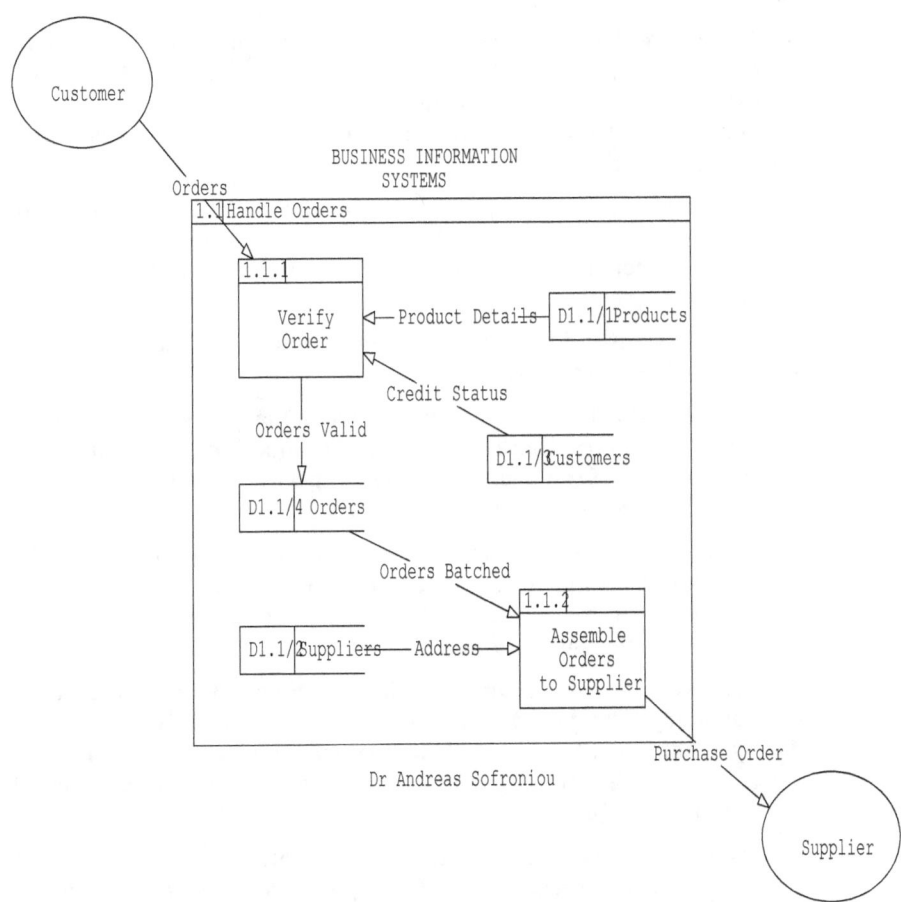

Each process in the top level DFD can be exploded to become a lower level DFD. Each process at the lower level will need to be related back to the higher level process, by giving the lower level process box an identification number which is a decimal of the high-level process. Thus, box number 2 is decomposed into 2.1, 2.2, 2.3, 2.4, and 2.5. Should it be necessary to go to a third level, 2.5 is decomposed into 2.5.1, 2.5.2, 2.5.3, 2.5.4, 2.5.5.

The lower level DFD is drawn within the boundary which represents the higher level process. All dataflows in and out of the higher level process must enter and leave the boundary. Datastores which are shown inside the boundary of the upper level, at the lower level DFD is shown outside the boundary.

Once the DFDs have been drawn and described, the Analyst has to decide whether a function should remain in the level shown, or identify lower level functions which are additions to the ones shown on the higher level processes.

To summarise the diagrammatic representation of an existing, or required system, identify the:

- External Entity. This involves a preliminary system boundary. Place the external entities outside the boundary, with dataflows into and out of the boundary, thus connecting the external entities with the processes inside the boundary.

- Inputs and the outputs (those arrows which represent the dataflows). What one expects in the normal course of any business. As the amount of dataflows increases invent logical groupings of inputs and outputs.

- Processes which represent the functions within the DFD boundary. The Analyst must remember that a process is triggered by a dataflow, the input of data which require a function. Once the process has undergone the transaction, the details are flowed out to be stored.

- Datastore, which can be the representative of a cupboard, a drawer, or a current system. The input of the data into a datastore can be on a temporary, or permanent basis. Whatever goes into a datastore must come out; otherwise the datastore will be the dead end of the information cycle.

USING THE METHODOLOGY

As computers get cheaper, many companies are finding that they can gain from operating systems. Additionally, many organisations find the benefit of using structured methodologies for the development of new systems. Structured analysis is useful in investigating the existing systems, be it manual or automated. The structured methods help with the understanding of the problems faced by a business and the obstacles in running a profitable environment.

Structured analysis definitely helps in deciding whether to install a computer and what parts of the systems to develop and interface the automated system with manual systems, clerical procedures other systems and perhaps suppliers' systems - customer companies' systems.

To answer such questions, maybe an initial study will assist in making a decision. Most certainly the answers will be focused on the questions of:

- What is wrong with the current situation?
- What improvements are possible?
- What are the benefits?
- Who will be affected by the new system?

In an organisation of any size, there is usually a stream of requirements from user departments for improvements in information technology services. While some of these requests can be met by improving the current systems, such as better response time, some may still bear further enhancements of the existing operating systems.

Many companies prefer to start from scratch and develop new systems and bring new ideas in running their computer systems. In such cases, the development of new systems is overdone. Many organisations find that the demand for new systems is several times greater than the resources allow.

An initial study (lasting from two days to a couple of weeks), will help to decide the route to be followed. The analyst should study the requests and meet with the managers to get the background and to begin to assess the costs and benefits of a possible new system.

It is useful to investigate the reasons for wanting to build a new system. It is fair to the analyst to remember that a new system may offer the opportunity to:

- Increase revenue,
- Avoid costs,
- Improve service.

By the end of the initial study, the analyst should be confident about the costs and the benefits resulting from a proposed system. The outcome of the initial study will be reviewed by the appropriate level of management or steering users group.

Once the go-ahead is authorised, a detailed study can begin. The detailed study builds on facts, current policies, functions, and methods of transacting a business.

The activities of the detailed study will include:

- Who the users of a new system will be,
- Functional areas considered,
- Collect views of objectives and preferences.

At this stage the building of a logical model of the current system starts and together with the refined estimates, a statement of possible increased revenue, avoidable costs, and improved services will be included in the detailed study.

As a result of this phase of the study, reviews will follow and a decision is usually made to continue the project to the next set of steps.

The definition of alternative should follow. Until the advent of structured methods, the offering of a 'menu' has not been a practical proposition, because the presentation of alternatives to users has been difficult. With structured analysis and designing, the presentation of alternative solutions involves the users in making a business decision and offers the system as an answer to what the user community requires.

The activities involved in the development of alternatives include:

- Deriving objectives from the current systems,
- Cataloguing of the new requirements,
- Developing a logical model of the new system,

Typically, the logical model by this stage consists of the overall DFD and the logical data structure. This logical model will be reviewed in detail with users and any feedback will be used to alter the documentation accordingly and will be incorporated in the design of the phase.

The analyst frequently acts as agent for the users in these phases, just like an architect will supervise the construction of a building, ensuring that the plans are being followed. The analyst will keep the logical model up-to-date, through design and implementation, especially the DFDs (data flow diagrams).

There are various steps which need to be taken in order to introduce the structured techniques into a systems development organisation, with consideration to the benefits expected, together with the problems that people experienced in using systems.

The main steps involved in implementing a structured methodology in a company are:

1. Reviewing the method used for projects.

   The amount of work involved in assessing the procedures used in systems development will vary greatly, depending on whether a formal structured methodology has been adopted, or whether the organisation has created its own ground rules.

   Any method based on structured analysis will specify a sequence of activities to be followed in creating a system, the products to be developed at each stage and the management controls to be applied. Almost any established method will, in general, specify the conduct of a feasibility study. Following a feasibility study, a detailed design, followed by coding and testing.

   If such a methodology is already used, check that:

   - It does not encourage pre-mature physical design. If so ensure that this is modified to allow for the logical stages to be introduced prior to entering the physical stage.

   - The methodology in existence does not subscribe to over-documentation - the exhaustive narrative details. The DFDs and data modelling can easily replace the excessive writing and descriptions.

   - The present method allows for top-down development. This point raises a more fundamental issue. That of the 'straight-line-approach'. Many systems engineers assume that a well-managed development project goes in a 'straight line', from the feasibility study to the analysis, through design into testing and users acceptance. The path of such a project can be completed by using a 'spiral' approach.

The spiral concept reflects the reality of the problems faced in systems development. At each progressing phase a skeleton is built, this is then logicalised and walked through to see how well the logical phases work and then reverse to put more details into the study. Thus, the project control needs to accommodate the delivery of sensible products; dataflow diagrams, data structures and functional analysis, rather than the completion of activities.

2. Establish standards for the use of a CASE (Computer-aided Software Engineering) tool.

A decision may have to be made to acquire a CASE tool. This is a good support for the Analyst's responsibilities in diagramming the system-to-be. It is very convenient to have a tool for diagrammatic representations for the maintenance and easy updating of diagrams and specifications in general.

CASE tools are progressing so quickly, the latest versions include the facilities for quick prototyping and transforming the descriptions to structured English and in turn to 4GLs coding.

3. The tools and techniques of structured systems analysis must be as simple and as realistic as possible. To use any system engineering techniques expertly needs experience; study and practice. While the rules and conventions can be learnt easily, the hardest thing appears to be at the logical level.

Whatever the difficulty, a DFD showing sequence of events improves the understanding of the users, thus the analyst's tasks become much easier. In analysis and design users are asked to think about problems at a higher level of abstraction and this can take time and persistence.

Apart from the fluency with the logical tools, the analysts need to become familiar with the emerging support software. If the ground rules for projects are to change, analysts will have to explain them to the users. Analysts need to be briefed on new methodology and think through its implications for users.

If structured development is to be used, the analysts must be thoroughly briefed on the concept and the implementation plan of each project with which they are concerned. The analyst, most certainly, must be able to criticise a design in the light of the structured methodology principles.

4. As the new structured techniques and approaches improve communication with users and involve them more in setting the direction of the project, they are welcomed by the user community. At the same time, the new ideas represent a change in the rules of developing systems, in a positive way, as the implications and benefits are clearly explained in the process of designing.

The communication with the users, as each 'structured' project starts, should cover the following points:

- Notation of the DFD,
- Concept of presenting a 'menu' of alternative systems for the users to consider,
- Briefing on the structured method,
- Warning on the participation and involvement required on the part of the users,
- Reassurance that the new method for system development does not impose more effort,

- **New project will not generate more paperwork for the users.**

In some companies, the users are trained to draw their own DFDs and their own descriptions in structured English. The analyst ought to encourage this, provided the individual user wants to go ahead with this. This concept, in many organisations, proved very beneficial, in as much as the communication difficulties experienced prior to this method, they just disappeared. The users felt as if they were guiding the project the way it suited them.

Where specific executives are assigned as members of the Users Committee, it is desirable that they should be trained in structure methodology. This will give them the ability to present the business, their point of view, and the requirements, subsequently defining them to the analyst. The Executives trained in structured analysis can be more informed critics of the logical models produced by the system engineering area.

With structured training, the users will be able to quantify most of the benefits that result from improved productivity and the better management time and resources.

The benefits from using structured systems analysis, from the system architecture point of view, are even more profound:

- **Users get a much more vivid idea of the proposed system from logical DFDs, than they do from narratives and excessive descriptions,**

- **Presenting the system in terms of logical DFD reduces the misunderstandings and issues,**

- Interfaces between the new system and existing systems are shown clearly by the DFD and the data model,

- Use of logical models eliminates duplications.

The benefits, of course, are not free from potential problems. The problems may be partly due to the change in working procedures and partly the result of the discipline imposed by the logical phases.

This type of problem can easily be reduced by:

- Introducing training to the users and the analysts as early in the project as possible,

- The effort and degree of detail required, especially in building the data model is often resisted. The consolation here is that, if the data are right in the first attempt, then less effort will be needed in the latter stages of development,

- Where structured English are introduced, programmers feel uneasy and often complaint that all fun is taken out of programming and that they become mere coders. The uneasiness goes away when the programmers see that structured systems give them more work to do, by bringing forward their responsibilities, during the designing stage.

- Introducing structured techniques for analysis, design and development, starting at any point in a project.

RAPID BUILDING METHOD

A quick method for building systems, using structured design techniques make for better systems, at lower costs, by providing techniques for detecting and correcting errors as early and as cheaply as possible.

Although quicker, it still means going through the structured analysis, designing, top-down development, structured coding and having structured walkthroughs. What it means, is that the system analyst tries to cut down the unproductive use of professional time by matching what is possible with what is worth doing.

To manage such steps requires a lot of experience in the whole system development lifecycle and at each step the following thoughts ought to be raised:

- The system being built is of a technically excellent status, but is this what the users want?
- The users were given what they asked, but could the Analyst have done so much more for them?

In approaching the quick way of developing a system the analyst needs good probing techniques. He or she must find out the factors which stand in the way of achieving the objectives. The factors which would be impacted by better, faster, richer information.

It is a fact, that unlike other business projects, system analysis cannot produce a model. In complex construction projects, a scale model is built and everybody concerned can get a vivid idea of what the final building will look and how their interests will be served.

In information technology this can be done by diagrammatic representation, demonstration of dataflow diagrams and screen prototypes.

'Boxes' as symbols are used as the tools of structured analysis in a DFD (Dataflow Diagram) form, where they fit together as a logical model of a system, at any level of detail.

The symbols involved are:

- External Entity (outside the boundary),
- Dataflow,
- Process (Each process within the boundary can be exploded),
- Datastore.

The quick building method relies heavily on the composition of Structured English, which in turn depends on the:

- Functional decomposition,
- Lowest level - decomposed DFD,
- Entity diagram,
- Descriptions.

The details extracted from all four above will 'sieve' into Structured English.

These in turn, have their own conditions and actions:

> IF condition - 1
>> THEN action - A
> ELSE (not condition - 1)
>> action - B.

In nested 'Ifs', using 'AND-IF', the following example may help:

> IF you need a holiday
>> AND-IF you can afford it
>>> AND-IF you have somewhere to go
>>>> THEN take a holiday
>>>> ELSE (you have nowhere to go)

As a rule of thumb, in writing Structured English please do not nest more than three levels.

The role of the analyst in all this is of great importance.

A well trained, ethical individual with about five years experience will be able to:

- Help in devising the system versions and speak for the users' interests,
- Explain the top-down development concept to the user community,
- Ensure management support for timely systems development,
- Exert pressure for frequent, full integration of sub-systems,
- Ensure that the sub-system is developed top-down,
- Act as the users' representative in accepting each version.

Based on the procedures standards defined in the next chapter, the Analyst will carry out an analysis of the present systems operations and identify the problems.

This exercise will include the:

- Computer system,
- Manual system
- Combination of both.

This stage will be followed by the specification of the required system where the requirements are consolidated and the chosen option is defined in detail. In parallel to this, the required data structure is created.

SYSTEMS MANAGEMENT

The majority of organisations recognise that the effective use of information is vital to their success. Successful companies build enormous knowledge bases that reside in their corporate files, their information centres and in the brains of their busy executives. This knowledge and experience is the organisation's power base and their competitive edge.

To remain competitive they must be able to find information at the right time, in the right place and in the format that is easy to use..

The management of the information systems must ensure:

- Availability of the information,
- Services that enable this,
- Effective use of technology,
- Supply of the skills and time needed.

When the IT department manages the information derived from the systems, effectively, the company in turn gains real value from information. The IT department and its management of information must maintain a leading position in the specialised world of commercial computing.

The IT department will certainly benefit by having a network of specialists providing knowledge, experience, and technical skills to suit most types of company demands.

In managing IT professionally, the benefits will include the:

- Capturing of the knowledge already in the organisation,
- Making this knowledge accessible to those running the company,
- Developing the appropriate strategic plans and systems,
- Protection of the information supplied by the systems,
- Accuracy and recoverability of all data,
- Recruitment, training, and developing the system analysts.

Instant access to corporate information means better decisions, reduced costs, and increased profits. To facilitate such a service, the IT department must work with a wide range of other departments and their staff. Many of the users are looking for help or advice from the information management area.

This means that the IT staff must be prepared to undertake all sizes of projects, their development, and the management of such systems. This entails a project management system which, together with the chosen methodology, will ensure the success of the information services.

MANAGEMENT OF PROJECTS

A project management system should be utilised on all sizeable projects undertaken. A Project Manager should be appointed, responsible for the agreement and delivery of project products to agreed deadlines throughout the project's lifecycle.

The main project management issues include:

- Proper user, staff and management training,
- Management commitment,
- Budgets,
- User and expert time,
- Identify key users,
- Schedule time for analysis and design,
- Establish metrics,
- Small teams.
- Testing implementation and handover to users.

The Project Manager should produce a weekly status report which will be provided one day prior to a weekly progress meeting.

This report will have the following format:

- Milestones, summary report of the current and previous status of milestones,
- Progress, a narrative of progress,
- Changes to the project baseline, including change notices,
- Issues, details reported for current week and the status of those previously reported,
- Variances in either time, or effort for any milestone,

- Resource usage for the week,
- External factors that may impact upon progress, but not within the control of the project management,
- Cost reports of any costs incurred during the week, excluding resource costs and known regular costs,
- Objectives and risks for the next period,
- Recommendations and issues for discussion.

The weekly meeting should take place between the:

- Users' Project Manager, or representative,
- System Project Manager, or representative.

During the project lifecycle, project issues can occur which require analysis, documentation and resolutions. Project issues fall into those that occur during the:

- Development and delivery of the system,
- Operational life of the system.

Any change to the requirements, or to any document once it has been formally agreed, is subject to the following change control procedures:

- A change control notice will be raised by the user requesting the change,
- An estimate of the impact of the change on the schedule and costing of the project will be prepared by the system Project Manager,
- The change details will be transmitted to the users representative for authorisation,
- If the change is authorised, then the change control notice will be annotated by the member of the project team, who implements the change to indicate that it has been completed. A copy will then be filed with the documentation affected,

- The documentation itself will be updated to reflect the change, with update pages sent to all nominated parties,
- All changes during the project, whether by the user, or system developer will be controlled by the IT project area.

Throughout the life of the project, reviews of critical documents are necessary. The procedures for review of these documents are as follows:

- All critical documents will be reviewed within the project team structure to ensure adherence to the project standards,
- The quality to be randomly selected and reviewed by the Assurance Manager,

In case of controlled documents, this will include a check that the documents have the following details:

- Document identification,
- Document name,
- Name of system Project Manager,
- Distribution list,
- Current version.

The strategy of the system acceptance will be defined by the user. The subsequent plan and test scripts will be based upon the standards. As part of a quality management system, a senior manager undertakes the auditing of the project. The quality auditor operates outside the design and builds team structures.

Before delivery of the system, a training schedule for the users will be agreed. Additionally, prior to any handing over, the system will be tested and should any problems arise, these will be reported and remedied before the users sign off.

With the state-of-the-art in logical analysis, the accelerated progress in technology, and the demand made on more systems development, the IT management find themselves increasingly occupied in the selection of larger number of specialised staff. Such is the great weight on IT managers, to fulfil new job responsibilities and to replace those who leave for greener pastures.

The vacancies for system analysts are constantly increasing, at such a rate that a new industry has developed. Additional to the traditional recruitment, the demand for the supply of contractors, mainly for systems analysis and programming, has increased in proportions. Agencies for freelancers are now deeply rooted as a service to IT.

The contracting analysts are in their thousands and agencies in their hundreds. The cost to the organisation for such a service is huge, often enough remuneration paid being higher than what the business directors are paid. Frequently more than the IT manager gets. With such numbers of candidates involved and an unknown expertise at that, the systems managers are faced with the additional responsibility of frequent interviews and uncertainty as to what kind of know-how they will obtain from contractors.

The agencies do not have the knowledge to scrutinise every systems analyst on their registers. It is a well known fact that the agents submit the CVs of individuals without even checking on the contractor's experience. The agencies arrange for the interviews between the company's managers and the freelancers over the telephone. For this kind of service the agencies receive between 20% and 40% of the contracting fees. The larger, established contracting agencies have a firm charge of 33% commission.

The IT management and their staff are faced with the overload of interviews. It is an under-estimated task. With all the pressures from within the systems areas, it is a wonder how systems can be developed and become operational within the quoted timescales and costs.

As an example (using the two extremes of the systems professions), the analysts, and programmers, it is of paramount importance to use the right techniques for interviewing systems staff. In hiring systems professionals, it must be remembered that an analyst is the person who keeps in touch with the users and the programmer is the one that builds the system.

The analyst must be an outgoing person, a good mixer - a person who can get on with other people, easily collect information, and must be a good systems representative. This is a psychological personality type of an extrovert thinker.

On the other extreme, bear in mind that the programmer has to decipher the documents the analyst produces, in order to start constructing the required system. This makes the programmer the psychological personality of an introvert sensation type.

There are many other types of professionals within systems development. The list includes designers, database administrators, operators, strategists, and a few more. In interviewing, therefore, the interviewer will be helped enormously if he/she makes a few notes beforehand regarding the type of person needed to fill in the responsibilities within the systems professions.

In interviewing, handing out a short narrative and asking the interviewee to turn it into diagrams and programming coding is not on. The candidate must be relaxed, made to feel wanted, important and then prompted to expand on items relevant to the vacancy.

Systems building is such a modern profession, its responsibilities and qualities are hardly known to psychologists, psychometrists, and professional recruiters. For instance, one cannot rely on aptitude testing alone, as there are no set rules. Experience in systems areas and knowing what is needed is the best guide and basis for the interview.

Within the various scales of recruitment are the newcomers to the professions of systems management: The graduates of IT 'hybrid' management and the MBAs, whose degree material is based on traditional management. I.T. logical analysis demands organisational experience gained within business functions relating to systems.

The young graduates of the first degree education can be recruited with the proviso that they get trained within the business parameters. It is true that the new universities in their computing sciences subjects cover methodologies, databases and programming, but the question still prevails; the extend of commercial experience embedded in the lecturers and their tutorials and those running the academic departments. Let it be stressed that this statement refers to the business computing and systems development in the commercial world.

Universities have progressed enormously in their research on artificial intelligence and other fields such as parallelism. The outside world still runs systems on mainframes and applications as required by the users. The modern construction of business systems and tools developed, suit the personalities and the abilities of those who use these applications.

Faced with such problems, the IT management pays a lot of attention to interviewing. After all, like any other recruitment, employing a human being (permanent or contractor) is still a big investment of time, costs, and other resources.

It must be added, that the interviewing techniques in commercial computing are applied to applicants for vacant positions, as well as the users who ask for new systems, the repairing of an existing one, or the extraction of the data based information.

Interviewing is the most commonly used way of acquiring basic concepts and requirements from the users. It is an activity that needs careful planning and execution. It is crucial to plan an interview to ensure that it is as productive as possible.

Whether interviewing an applicant for a vacancy, or a user for his/her requirements, it is worthwhile bearing the following in mind:

- Ensure that the interviewee is prepared for the interview,
- Notify the subject to be covered,
- The time and location of the interview,
- Probable length of the interview,
- Ensure that a room is ready, away from the interviewee's workplace, thus minimising distractions,
- Make the interviewee comfortable with the computing terminology and jargon,
- Build a rapport, listen, and show interest.

As an interviewer, practise the art of relaxation on you and then apply the technique to the candidate. Remember that the users' interviewees may offer details on what they think you want to know. A good analyst will steer the discussion to the domain of interest, whereas a job applicant will be nervous, anxious and feel as if on the receiving end.

PROJECT CONTROL IN DEVELOPING SYSTEMS

Businesses have problems which they need to solve. They, also, have requirements which altogether enable the smooth running of their environment. To establish the appropriate running of the business organisation, projects need to be set.

An organisation is probably undergoing significant changes. Changes span functional boundaries, case conflict, and concern and present a major risk to the business and those managers responsible for the development of systems. Many companies are now adopting a project-based approach to managing the change of systems and their development.

Managers of today and of the future, require skills in managing projects. These skills are supplementary to the line management skills. A company needs to enhance business planning and control structures to explicitly link system implementation to business led projects and programmes.

A project in information technology is a temporary situation within the working groups (the system users) and the computing management, with the objective of delivering a product. The resulting product relies on the project progress and how it is approached in its scope to deliver.

For a project to be successful it needs:

- Management at all levels,
- Team building and staff motivation,
- Planning and controls,
- Quality standards to follow,
- Communication between users and management,
- Objectives and scope,
- Adequate skills and experienced resources,
- Explicit documentation and training.

Unlike existing systems operational management, where one deals with established computer services, project management encounters the unfamiliar, new problems and needs for change.

In managing a project, a list of activities will not be enough. The project must be product-based. A methodology needs to be followed, procedures to be applied. The appropriate procedures, therefore, give the advantage of common standards being applied to the management of all projects, with directional emphasis to meeting the corporate objectives.

Always remembering that a system is built with quality and that the application of the procedures and techniques must be flexible and practical:

- For the users,
- To fulfil a process,
- Benefit the business function.

Project management supports the implementation of the business strategies with explicit link to the development plan. This provides management with the ability to react swiftly and efficiently to any changes, to understand the project stages and steps in hand and their relationship with each other. It, also, provides an effective way of controlling costs and resources at all levels.

The appropriate analysis and design methodology will assist the project team members to concentrate on the system components to be produced. It enables the management and the analysts to identify and clearly define all the development phases. It is, also, a significant contributor to quality, better estimating, and planning.

This means that a systems manager and his/her team members need to establish project control standards, which will specifically include:

1. Purpose,

2. Scope,

3. Input,

4. Planning,

5. Progress control.

    1. Purpose:

The purpose of the project control standards is to define the standard to be used within system development for managing the project in terms of project planning and progress control.

The objectives of project management being:

- Establish clear objectives and scope for a project,
- Ensure roles and responsibilities are well defined and understood,
- Break work down into schedules and deliverables,
- Plan how an individual project will achieve the implementation of the required end product within a progressively refined and agreed schedule and budget.

A project control framework is necessary within which project management skills and techniques are exercised.

2. Scope:

This standard addresses Project Control in a new system development environment, i.e. a multi-team situation with Team Leaders and an overall Project Manager.

It covers the planning of each phase for each team and its members and the progressing of those plans.

3. Input:

The inputs will vary with the size and stage of development:

- Terms of Reference (ToR, for a new project) and Project Initiation Document (PID),

- Key documentation from earlier phases (for an existing project)

- Procedures manual

4. Planning:

The following steps describe a team leader's project control, carried out at the start of a project, or when rescheduling (as a result of supplying more tasks, or changing estimates).

- Task Identification. A source of information for this will be the overall project plan and the activities listed.

- Estimating. Estimating for project control planning is carried out using the bottom-up approach, starting with the steps involved and building upwards. When all tasks have been identified and estimated, an overall schedule can be drawn, which accounts for resource constraints, deadlines and overheads.

- Scheduling. The basics of scheduling are to take the information from task identification, sizing, and resource allocation and to build a schedule which meets the necessary timescales.

5. Progress Control:

The Project Control system and progress meetings are the principal mechanisms for monitoring and controlling the progress of a project.

- **Progress Meetings.** Aside from the informal contact maintained between a team leader and team members, each person should receive a regular progress meeting, on a one-to-one basis. Also, each team leader should meet with the project manager on a similar basis.

- **Team Meetings.** A regular weekly meeting of all team members is important, in order to maintain communication and to resolve issues where input is required.

- **Outstanding Issues.** As projects progress, design issues may emerge which require a solution. At the end of the development, any loose ends not resolved can be passed to the support team for future enhancements to the system.

- **Rescheduling.** Even the best planned project may have its scope changed by changes in requirements, or late design changes. Changes of this type can cause disruption which outweighs the benefits they provide, so it is important to keep them to a minimum.

SYSTEMS DEVELOPMENT PROCEDURES

The system specification procedures form the basis within the conventional business environment as these sets out the standards for system development. They describe a step by step approach to developing and implementing computer systems. They define the documents to be produced, the controls to be applied and the tasks to be performed.

The intention is that these procedures be applied flexibly. On the other hand, the phases are designed for sequential development, with the output from one phase being the input to the next, all leading to the eventual implementation of the system. Project plans should be drawn up to suit the particular project and then adhered to.

The procedures define the paths that will be followed in projects set up to develop computer systems. A project is, thus, described in terms of its major divisions (Phases), its Control Points, the Activities that are accomplished in each phase, and the tasks that go to make up those activities.

A project starts with an initiation and ends with a review and user training. The Project Initiation Document (PID) will incite the feasibility study and the terms of reference. The review will include the report to the users and the appropriate steps for the system training and the training manual distributed to all the users involved in the running of the system-to-be.

Otherwise, the project has the following phases:

- Business Analysis: Users' business Problems and Requirements and the initial top level Dataflow Diagram.

- Systems Analysis: System Proposal, Functional Decomposition, Dataflow Diagram, Logical Data Structure and Process Descriptions,

- Design Options: Technical Design Options,

- Functional Analysis: Process Model, Detailed Dataflow Diagram and Process Descriptions,

- Data Analysis: Data Model, Entity Life History,

- Physical Design/Build, System Specification, Program Code.

The system development lifecycle, in outlining the activities to be followed and the tasks to be carried out in a project, provides the framework for planning and defining a project.

The development lifecycle does not ensure that projects will meet a particular level of quality, nor does it ensure that work carried out will be both, efficient and effective. That is a matter of how people perform and it is the goal of project management to make sure that conditions exist for them to be efficient and effective.

The framework of the lifecycle with its different phases, offers some guidance on when project management should be applied. Each phase has a beginning, middle, and end. Project management procedures are ongoing and required to fit in with the dimensions of the workday and reporting cycles.

Project management is a series of activities that are carried out during a project by the leader:

- Planning,
- Estimating,
- Monitoring,
- Reporting,
- Quality control,
- Resource allocation,
- Communication.

The performance of any computer department can only be judged by the service given to the system users. This means a variety of business changes through projects. It involves people and the experience they carry with them. Experience in system building when a company needs it most; when this type of people, the best in the organisation is in short supply and great demand. They are usually, therefore, not available when needed for a critical new project - to develop the long awaited system.

SYSTEMS SPECIFICATION

The System Specification starts as systems analysis and is not completed until programming begins. A standard is required for conducting systems design because a uniform approach is needed across all projects to ensure understanding and consistency.

The standard outputs are required as input to programming activities. The systems specifications, therefore, need to be written in a rigorous and consistent manner to ensure that all user requirements are catered for and all business processing is completely and accurately defined and documented.

The following may be input to system specification:

- Current, systems documentation and specifications,

- Users' requirements documentation and proposals,

- System proposal from system analysis phase,

- Process descriptions, dataflow diagrams and layouts from the functional analysis phase,

- Minutes of meetings with users.

The System Specification is the phase where the lowest level dataflow diagrams and descriptions from process analysis are pulled together.

PROCESS ANALYSIS

The aim is to reach a detailed logical design sufficient for all specification work. A standard is required for conducting process analysis because a uniform approach is needed across all projects. It concentrates on processes rather than data. Thorough process analysis encourages understanding of the system and user environment. The outputs from the process analysis are required for the system design processes.

There can be many inputs into process analysis depending on the nature and complexity of the project. The following may be input to process analysis:

- Systems documentation and specifications from the current system,

- Users' requirements and proposals

- Decomposition of dataflow diagrams.

The dataflow diagram is a powerful input to design because it identifies the data flows, data stores and processing involved. The technique is top-down; an overview followed by increasingly lower levels of detail.

SYSTEM REVIEWS

The purpose of a review is to define the process for understanding what is required: Also as a method for checking the quality of work throughout the systems development lifecycle.

The objectives of holding a review of a piece of work are to:

- Ensure the work meets its requirements,
- Trap errors as early as possible,
- Provide a focus on outstanding issues which lie in the pathway to completion of a given task,
- Check adherence to standards.

It is clear that in practice it would not be appropriate to subject all outputs to the same level of review and several variants of the review process are required.

The different levels of review allow for the:

- Importance of the review material,
- Authority of the attendees,
- Level at which the review is documented,
- Formality with which the review is held.

PHYSICAL DESIGN

Physical design converts the results of process and data design into a computer solution for implementation and defines the computer/clerical interface. This is evaluated against the requirements and amended as appropriate.

The scope of the physical design is to cover the technical design of application systems. It concentrates on the design of the system processes, rather than the design of databases.

The following may be input to systems design:

- Current systems documentation and specifications,
- Users' requirements and solutions,
- System proposal from analysis phase,
- Process descriptions, dataflow diagrams and layouts from functional analysis phase.

Requirements often change during the design phase and new ones emerge. In addition, it often raises more questions requiring further analysis. Therefore, the final design may only be arrived at through several iterations of logical and physical design.

QUICK DATAFLOW DIAGRAMMING

Dataflow diagrams (DFDs) are used for process analysis, to show the logical:

- System processes, hierarchy and their relationships,
- Datastores, the system's data 'at rest',
- Data flows, the system's data 'in motion' between two processes, or between a process and a datastore.

To present a complete system description, additional documentation is necessary for each flow, each datastore, and each process.

It is the DFD which structures the analysis process and drawing the DFD helps the analyst to:

- Deal with the information collected during data gathering, in an orderly manner,
- Avoid being overwhelmed by detail and losing sight of the overall picture,
- Document the proposed system in a convenient format as input to design,
- Communicate with users.

PROGRAM DESIGN

Before they are coded, programs need to be designed. There needs to be a structure which shows how and where the processes diagrammed in the DFD and described in the System Specification are to be performed.

Structured English is used to represent the design. This is a simplified form of English, presented in defined manner. Within the structure so formed, normal English is used, although in as succinct a form as possible.

The relevant systems specification proceeds to a program design ready for coding.

To enable this, the following inputs are necessary:

- Decomposition diagram,
- DFDs at the program or transaction level,
- System specification,
- System flowchart,
- Data structure diagram.

A program design which is structured is easier to maintain and understand. The structuring of the design means principally that the design should be driven by the flows of input and output data.

The program designer or programmer should arrange for regular program and code Walkthroughs with another programmer/designer.

The walkthrough session should check:

- Adherence to programming standards,
- That the code matches the design structure,
- The code performs the processing defined in the system specification,
- Database accessing is correct.

Program designing and programming in general, requires disciplined management since this needs clearly defined objectives to fulfil the overall project.

Project management must, therefore, ensure that the investment of resources, time, and effort are fully justified and fulfilled. This includes program definition and the setting up of efficient structures. Whatever the requirements, experience is of major importance in helping and controlling programming

OVERALL OBJECTIVES

As organisations strive to increase productivity, to reduce costs, to shorten cycle times, to improve product and service quality, so the demands made on systems for modifications and for new information increase. Being able to make better decisions based on quality information and having the flexibility to respond to new opportunities increasingly, depends on having the right systems in place at the right time.

Applications developed based on older technologies may well not meet current requirements in some or many areas, such as:

- Functionality,
- Ease of use,
- Data access,
- Maintainability,
- Flexibility,
- Robustness,
- Costs.

With the wide range of application environments and building blocks now available, it is still possible to have an affordable system designed and built to meet specific business requirements. This gives the flexibility and control to define the system the way the users want it and then to change and adapt the system to support the business over coming years.

Computer-aided Software Engineering (CASE) tools address the application design stage. For business systems they can be extremely useful to assist in the design of both, the application and the data structure.

Rapid Application Development (RAD) techniques incorporate a series of steps which business people and Information Technology professionals work through together to develop a prototype of the application representing the business process before full scale development.

The objectives of analysis is to understand what a particular area of the business does and how information is exchanged, created and modified by business processes.

With a clear understanding of the information needs of a business area, the system engineer can determine which business activities to automate and then develop those systems so they meet end user requirements.

The design helps users move from a logical representation of 'what' a given system is to perform, into the physical specifications for 'how' the system will actually be implemented.

In order to handle the complex nature of a system, it is often helpful to break down the processes and data of the system into manageable pieces. Decomposition diagrams are an easy way to partition the data and process requirements of the system, by analysing and application, refining high level business processes into lower level processes. These processes can then be broken down further until the analyst reaches a level of detail where a process can best be described in terms of its procedural logic.

The analysis stage is unique in its approach to integrating the process model with the data model. The analyst can build the application data model by defining, one at a time, the data model for each individual process.

Dataflow diagrams can help describe how a business area or system functions. They show how data flows into and out of the business area or system, how processes transform data and the external agents (recipients/sources) that interface with the system.

Entities are the subjects of information (people, places, things) about which a business needs to keep data. An entity diagram provides a graphic way of describing the data requirements of a system and how they interrelate. The entity diagram, also, helps describe and characterise the relationships among these entities.

COMPUTER-AIDED SOFTWARE ENGINEER (CASE)

In many Information Technology (IT) departments, the complexity of applications often dictates that development responsibilities be divided among members of a project team. The ability to share information is a fundamental requirement for systems development tools.

Such tools, Computer-aided Software Engineer (CASE - some system engineers describe them as 'System', instead of 'Software') tools are designed to offer unequalled flexibility in combining and reconciling the work of multiple users. The analyst can selectively consolidate and separate, either whole, or partial encyclopaedias, or selected objects and maintain multiple encyclopaedias for different projects or users.

For an IT department to be a valued contributor to the company's success, its staff must be supplied with tools to respond effectively to business opportunities, where CASE tools can assist in the full life cycle of the applications development.

Applications which reduce costs, add value, and show effectiveness. For IT to be a valued contributor in business, its functions, and service to users must be highly adaptive, in planning, manufacturing, products design, marketing, and the overall company culture. To succeed in such concepts, IT conducts an inter-departmental analysis of its information systems, to assess its assets and capabilities.

As part of the new concepts, IT will bring forward a long range strategic plan for business systems. Evolve from a business system planning to an overall technical architecture planning approach. Tools, including CASE, are the key to the success of the overall technical architecture.

From the user perspective, the analysis of problems is critical. Detailed analyses of the operating systems, the manual systems, and the functional relationships will serve the purpose of the overall architecture. A CASE tool is highly instrumental, in being able to present the numerous applications to management and users and to gain consensus among the staff.

One of the strengths of the CASE tool is its ability to hold information, definitions, and comments. With a user-friendly tool, the analyst finds it easier to start and modify the diagrams. The users understand what the IT is doing. Pictures generated out of the tool are shown to the users for consensus and where necessary the diagrams get back into the tool to redraw.

The tool makes it easy. Diagrams are redrawn quickly and using the tool causes the analysts and users to question the analysis more. The result is a better quality system.

The CASE tool will prompt the analyst to begin with a decomposition of the areas that are involved and then a global data model which can be used as the starting point for the data model side of the project. These are explained to the users. In doing so, the design tool makes things easier. The analyst can move things around on the screen, which encourages modular design techniques.

As explained, the IT project team is responsible for the research and development of the advanced concepts and technologies in support of the company's information systems. The IT department is not only responsible for the traditional data administration duties, but also for the introduction of the CASE tools and the building up of the encyclopaedia.

CASE tools are a fairly new technology and systems engineers are still finding many ways to implement the potentials offered. Some CASE tools are design to be modular with separate tools for planning, analysis, and design and application generation. These tools can work together as a single integrated product, or separately as individual ones.

At the end of the day, no matter what anyone may say, a CASE tool, or any product may fail the IT department and the business as a whole, unless a properly documented system requirements specification is produced. A specification upon which everything will depend - to deliver what the user asked.

By now, all the phases, starting from the Project Initiation Document (PID), right through to the required analysis, the users' problems and requirements cataloguing, their solutions and the specification of the required system, all are complete. The next step is for the users to sign off this phase of the module, prior to starting on the building of the system.

The reader will appreciate that the volume of the documentation of the complete study of this fictional module may consist of more than one thousand pages. In view of this, only a few examples are selected as extracts of the system requirement specification. The full documentation of a module such as the example presented usually takes a small team of people a few months to complete.

Therefore, only one example of each one of the following is included in this book:

- Functional Decomposition Diagram and Report,
- Data Model Subset Diagram and Components,
- Data Inventory,
- Dataflow Diagrams Set and Descriptions,
- Functions,
- Transactions,
- Events,
- Problems and Requirements Catalogue,
- Solutions,
- Menu and Screens Reports.

Once all above are inserted in the CASE tool, the automatic outputs, included in the specifications, individually show the listing of all the components, within each picture, with the appropriate descriptions for each component. Every one of the components is associated to each other.

It is hard to imagine business today without information systems. Information Technology in general is an important part of business and everyday life. It has become very important for individuals and organisations, in the ability to compete, perform and prosper.

As a support structure and as a tool for business, systems can deliver a number of significant benefits. Costs can be reduced, productivity increased, services improved and profits enhanced.

People at the sharp end of business want a better understanding of the way that systems are developed and function. It is hoped that in this book systems issues are explained and that the I.T. logical analysis helps people to comprehend the broad aspects of technologies available to assist in achieving personal and business objectives.

Systems ought to be about enabling business and personal change.

COMMERCE AND THE INTERNET

The term 'Electronic Commerce' (e-commerce) is commonly used to mean doing business electronically. It is the paperless exchange of critical business information between companies and their suppliers, government departments, financial institutions, customers and companies, even within organisations.

Business today sees the electronic commerce as a way to streamline operations, reach new markets, and serve their clients more efficiently. It can often be a catalyst for business change through business process re-engineering. A streamlined new process nearly always entails some degree of automation. Since many business processes cut across boundaries between departments, divisions and even companies, electronic commerce is a natural way to automate these processes.

A popular method of communication for exchanging data is Electronic Data Interchange (EDI). EDI may be defined as the 'exchange of standardised structured information between computer systems'.

EDI lends itself to the exchange of high volumes of information in a fixed format agreed by industry groups. This includes invoicing and payments, retail point-of-sale, bank transactions and manufacturing inventories. Because information is created and transferred electronically, there is no need for paperwork. This eliminated the need for re-keying data, which saves labour, speeds up processes and reduces details errors. Significant cost savings and reduced lead times can be achieved.

Processes can be automated and re-structured so that maximum operational efficiency is obtained. EDI operates by direct connection between users and over private and public data networks, ensuring privacy and security. As it uses highly structured formats, transmission speeds can be increased and overall costs reduced.

An e-commerce business solution relies on a network to act as a conduit for the transfer of data. Often, a 'value-added network' from a commercial provider is used, to provide the infrastructure required to transfer data securely and reliably among trading partners.

Until a few years ago, the Internet was not well known. One could scarcely have predicted the impact it would have on the world of systems and computers communications.

From its inception in the 1960s, the Internet evolved into a global network of business, academic and government computers. In recent years, businesses and individual users have recognised its potential as a way of communicating; by exchanging electronic mail, transferring files, accessing information services and communicating via bulletin boards, computer conferencing, and social interfacing.

The communication has been accompanied by the emergence of a part of the Internet known as the World Wide Web (WWW), which allows information to be presented in a graphical format; incorporating text, images, video and sound.

Any user with a suitable facility such as the latest mobile telephone, laptops, notebooks, personal computer (PC) can access the Web through a connection to the Internet using the wi-fi facility, broadband and the normal telephone land line.

Businesses are now setting up electronic shop-fronts and information sites on the Web and starting to realise the immense potential for reaching a global audience.

However, this open access to the vast storehouse of information raises a number of issues. The openness of the Internet leads to concerns over security. The Internet is a public set of networks that interconnect and are not inherently secure. As a consequence, there is a demand for effective software security tools known as 'firewalls'. These act as a secure gateway to limit outsiders' access to a company's data systems and provide control over staff access to the Internet.

Companies and individuals are reluctant to transmit and exchange sensitive details over the Internet, such as credit card information. The problem is now being addressed by developing effective encryption tools. The combination of firewalls and encryption will enable the realisation of the Internet's full commercial potential.

One genuine limiting factor on Internet usage is data transmission speeds. Although these have improved in recent years, for most users they remain painfully slow. It takes a few minutes to download and read even a basic Web page. Transferring large data files is often impracticably slow. These and other management issues associated with security, training and implementation, should be taken into account when considering the Internet as part of a personal or business strategy.

END

SECTION TWO

RISKS

Andreas Sofroniou

CONTENTS: PAGE:

1 RISKS LOGICAL ANALYSIS

1.1 PROGRAMME MANAGEMENT

Programme Management may have many responsibilities, but the most important of all is the ability to identify and positively execute plans to manage the risks threatening the objectives.

Through a process of structured interviews and plans the Assessment Analysis is used to highlight the specific Events which may turn into Risks. During the interviews Assessment Analysis is used to capture the key Events from the interviewees.

In turn, the Assessment Analysis provides a life-cycle process, which highlights the primary prioritisation of the risks. In large, complex, and critical programmes, it is essential that a true prioritised report is available so that the imminent threats can be managed first.

The process commences by identifying the most important events which may become threats to a project. These are given priority, support and management expertise. Once the prioritisation exercise is completed, the participating people are notified and subsequently interviewed to bring out and capture any possible concerns they may have.

Within a programme, projects are prioritised to ensure that those most critical to the programme's success are given priority to scarce resources.

1.2 RISK MANAGEMENT METHODOLOGY

The I.T. Risks Logical Analysis allows the capture of collective knowledge and expertise from those involved on the project, in a form that facilitates the communication of Events, Assessments and the pro-active management of risks. This method can be applied to any type of project, or programme.

In essence, this is the mechanism by which the functions of programmes and projects are held together as a result of the principles operating within the I.T. risk analysis methodology.

This is the systematic approach to the varied Events, their Assessments, and the consequential risks relating to or consisting of a system. Methodical in procedures and plans, these are addressed to those involved and deliberating within the parameters of their systems development responsibilities.

The results being dependable on the interaction and the mutual or reciprocal action which encourages those involved in the programmes and projects to communicate with each other and to work closely with a view to solving the threatening Events before they impact on the development of the system.

The individuals involved maintain a generic approach, which relates and characterises the whole group of those involved in assessing the Events and attacking the threatening ones before they become Risks to the development of the system. The end result being the avoidance of apparent problems within the pre-defined users' systems requirements.

This is enabled by following the I.T. Risk Management methodology. The system architects and the risk management practitioners simply follow the approved body of systems development methods, rules and management procedures employed by their organisation. For practical or even ethical reasons, it must be noted that with such a philosophy, it is seldom possible to fulfil all requirements of very large organisational systems.

As such, the I.T. Risk Management methodology is administered in applications; putting to use such techniques and in applying the Risk Management principles in the development of various applications will involve numerous and varied activities. A concrete issue in developing new applications is the problem of communication among the people involved, the motivation constantly needed for *generic* work, the ability to *interact systematically* and in using a structured systems *methodology*.

1.3 RISK MANAGEMENT CYCLE

The concept being a simple one as shown in the diagram below:

Risk Management Cycle

The I.T. Risk Management methodology was developed by the author whilst employed by *PsySys Limited,* over a period of some thirty years. The methodology was used for PsySys' international clients, from 1982 onwards. The idea of a structured approached to organisational problems proved beneficial to customers and users who integrated the full process with other methodologies, such as Structured Systems Analysis and Designing methods and Project Management procedures.

1.4 INTEGRATION OF METHODOLOGIES

The comprehension of how to integrate the three methodologies can be achieved, simply by following the concept as shown on the following diagrammatic representation:

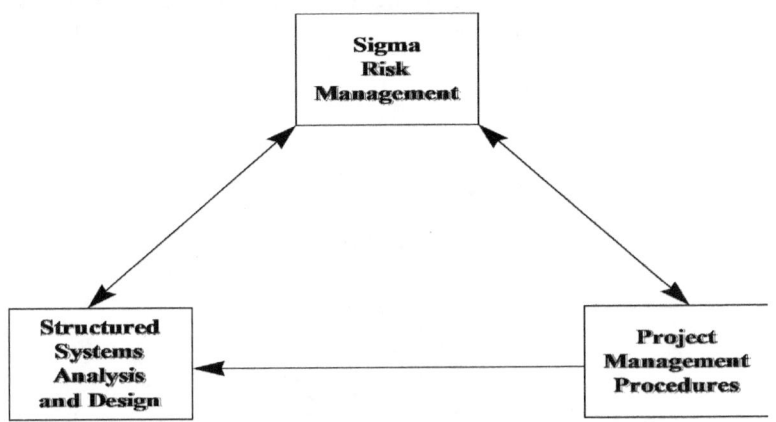

Integration Of Methodologies

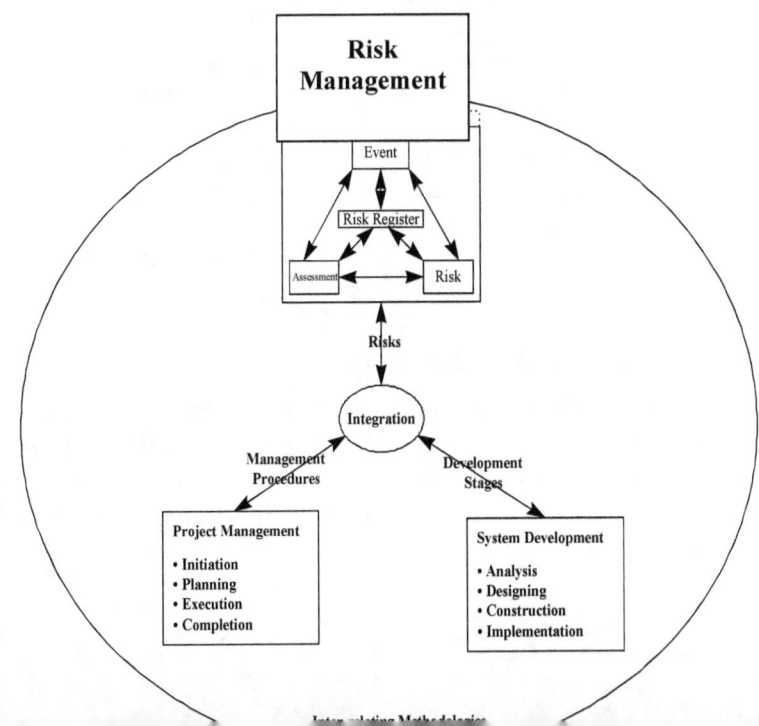

1.5 INTER-RELATIONSHIP

The various steps included in each of the methodologies are named in the next diagram. Or, to a further extent, the various stages of system development and the steps taken to manage projects and adopt the risk management cycle, are shown on the next page:

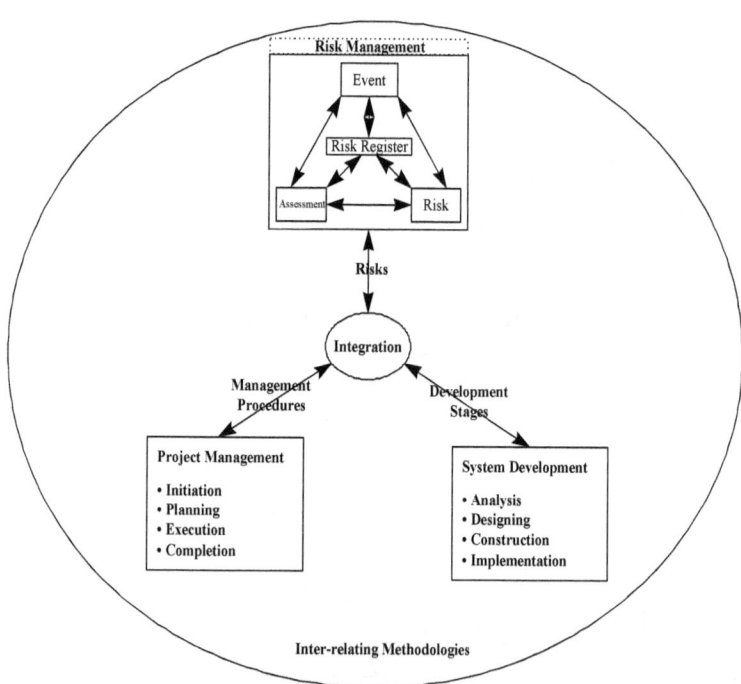

Inter-relating Methodologies

1.6 MANAGING THE RISK PROGRAMME

It is basic business sense to identify, assess, manage, and monitor risks that are significant to the fulfilment of an organisation's business objectives. In recent years businesses have been transformed by, and are in many cases heavily dependent on I.T.

The financial consequences of a breakdown in controls or a security breach are not only the loss incurred, but also the costs of recovering and preventing further failures. The impact is not only financial: it can affect adversely reputation and brand value as well as the business' performance and future potential.

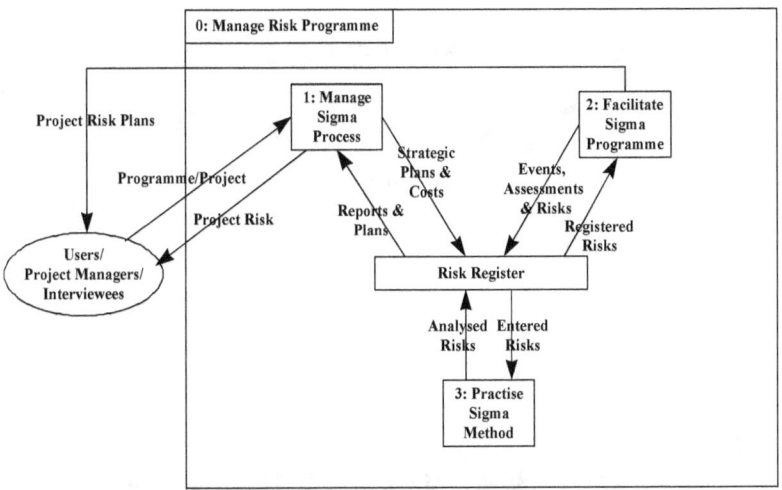

(The term *'Sigma'* used in the process boxes in some diagrams is based on the *PsySys* method of Risk Management.)

1.7 IMPACT ON BUSINESS

Organisations can regard inadequate system development as a significant risk, and where directors feel that this may be the situation in their businesses, they may need to ask tough questions of themselves and their management teams. Systems development and their risks is an issue that companies may need to recognise should regularly be on their agenda, and not delegated to I.T. technicians.

Business in the past was primarily confined to assessment of the risk surrounding fire, flood, and Acts of God. In business today we have become dependent on information systems. Failure to build computer systems as required by the users has a major impact on our business to function. The inability of companies to provide adequate systems can cause potential problems to customers, suppliers, employees and an all round havoc to information.

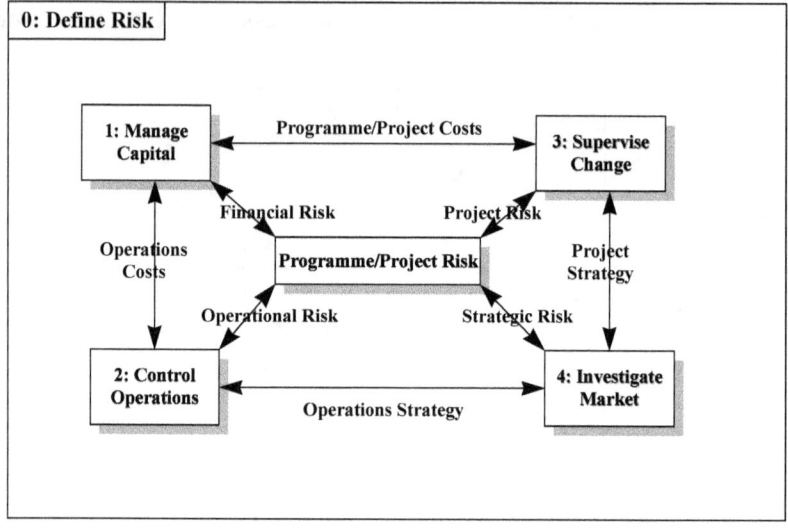

Programme/Project Risk: One Component Of The Total Business Risk.

2 RISK ANALYSES

2.1 ASSESSMENT OF RISKS

Fundamental to the creation of a Risk Management system is the assessment of the risks (Risks Analysis) to your business and the potential loss that could accrue if things go wring. Risk Assessment software tools are available in the market, which can be used by consultants, or by internal staff. What is important is the ability to assess the risk to your business and the cost to protect it against the risk. The end result is that you have to make the valued judgement on the amount the business spends on the implementation and the monitoring of a risk policy.

Products and systems are available to counter the threats and risks that have been identified. There is a wide range of options available, but remember that anything chosen will require expertise to design and complete a system, taking into account how the various solutions will inter-react with each other. Like all things to do with I.T., the design and implementation of systems' risk solutions is only as good as the people installing them.

2.2 COMMUNICATION

The MOST important factor in the success of any management style is the ability to communicate with each other, one to one or in groups of people. The art of communication is just as important to the whole process of the management of risks. More so where the risks identified have become a threat because of the problem of human communications.

This is where the appointment of an experienced and trained Risk Practitioner is worth the effort put into securing such individual/s.

2.3 RISKS MANAGEMENT PRACTICE

A trained Practitioner will have enough knowledge to run and maintain the system, as well as ample experience to be able to communicate with all levels of employees, hold meetings, and ensure the plans executed.

In brief and as the diagram on the next page shows, the Practitioner will be responsible for the complete Risk Management cycle.

2.4 RISK MANAGEMENT CYCLE

In analysing risks, certain counter measures may have to be looked into. The mechanisms for safeguarding the construction of your information system are by managing risks and avoiding the threat of failing to build the required system.

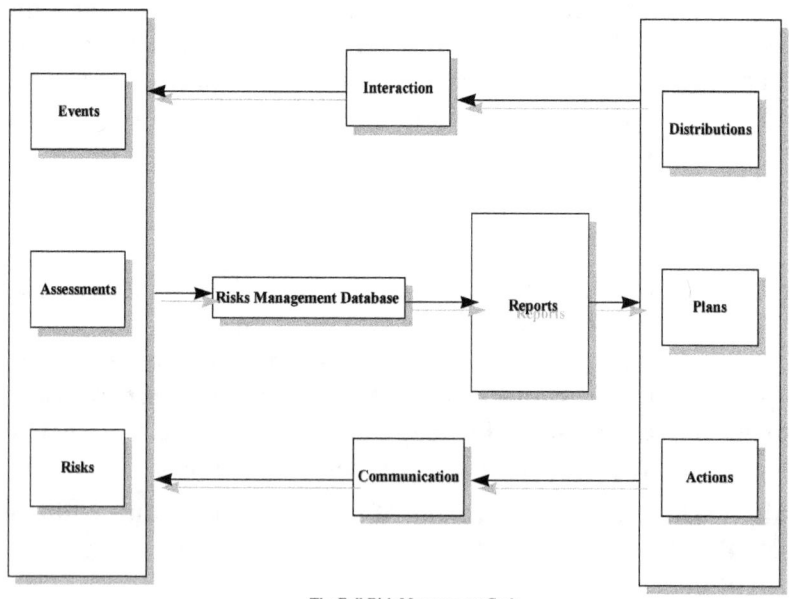

The Full Risk Management Cycle

2.5 INTERNET COMMERCE

Internet Commerce is a key component of the Global Networked Business model, providing a company's customers and partners with end-to-end solutions to conduct business transactions and exchange of information.

As a background, probably the main driver for building the Internet Global Commerce model has been the need for continuous business improvement, leading to cost savings achieved by changes in the supply chain.

Global businesses and manufacturing techniques now ensure that the business works twenty-four hours, by seven days, by fifty-two weeks basis, which can only be effectively managed by the integration of computer systems on the equivalent global basis. The computer industry is reacting by introducing further interoperability between computer systems with the introduction of new software and bigger capacity technological devices.

Further on, the Internet, this network of networks stretches around the world and makes it possible for every computer to connect to every other computer. It is the biggest network in the world.

2.6 WORLD WIDE WEB

Often confused with the Internet, this is the most widely used means of publishing and accessing information that is stored on the computers that are connected to the Internet.

The web allows you to link to many sites on the Internet. The basic concept is the page or collection of screens that it displays on your monitor. Within each page are links to related pages and other web sites. Each of these links is known as a hypertext link.

The web was originally used for text links only, but as it was further developed multimedia links were added. The web now contains pictures, audio and video links. With the addition of sound and graphics the web soon became the most popular way of linking to resources on the Internet.

Most organisations are worried by threats presented in using the web. Viruses are one of the main concerns, although these are unlikely to occur in normal surfing, except perhaps where Word and Excel documents are downloaded. Unauthorised access by outsiders is another.

Many organisations are also concerned about the employees wasting time surfing inappropriate web sites. To overcome this problem some companies choose to install a Content Security product that checks for ratings, profanity, and legal disclaimers.

2.7 BUSINESS CASE

The business case for justifying the expenditure on implementing a Risk Management system and the practising procedures to go with it in the early days of system development was more a leap of faith than a carefully evaluated financial case, and in many cases this may still be so.

Consultancy assignments and studies show that only a small percentage of organisations world-wide are taking this subject seriously. It is hoped that the information in this book will encourage you to review the Risk Management policy within your company.

2.8 GLOBAL NETWORKED BUSINESS

A Global Networked Business is a company, of any size, whose networked infrastructure and use of technology speeds up the process of communication, and the sharing of knowledge-between prospects, customers, employees, partners and suppliers.

A Global Networked Business uses networks and information technology to:

- Empower people to use and share information and to act more decisively,

- Transcend traditional barriers – including geographic, financial or organisational barriers,

- Increase responsiveness to customer needs and business opportunities,

- Compete more effectively in the global marketplace,

- Enables its customers, partners, employees, and suppliers to access information, resources and services in ways that work best for them.

2.9 IMPLEMENTATION OF RISK STRATEGY

The success, or failure, surrounding a Risk Management Strategy depends almost entirely on people, those who are designing and developing it and those who are expected to implement it. If the system is designed in such a way as to be too complicated to understand and comply with, or in such a way that makes it almost impossible to do ones job, then it will be rejected by those who should implement it.

Implementation of the policy is likely to involve modification of employment contracts. Monitoring the passage of information in and out of the organisation will involve human communication as well as technological means of communicating, such as the analysis of e-mails sent by employees, which can infringe their human rights, as can monitoring which sites are accessed on the Internet.

Care in selecting those who implement the Risk Management principles can substantially influence the level of confidence attained. The programmes require parameters to be set and therefore the level of understanding of your business requirements and the software will influence policies success or otherwise.

The communication exercise to the employees is probably the most important part of the implementation. If left to the I.T.

department, it may be delivered in seem-technical language or in terms of the needs of the business, rather than in terms and language to which employees can relate. Failure to allocate sufficient budgets to this area can put the success of a risk management policy in jeopardy. It is also important to remember to include training in this area as part of the employees' induction.

Adoption of a Code of Ethics can be a useful adjunct to the process, as can the use of an external communication company.

3. METHODOLOGY EXPLAINED

3.1 PROGRAMME OBJECTIVES

It is a fact that most large, complex projects and programs fail to meet their planned objectives and as a consequence, most organisations are undertaking one or more aggressive programs at any point in time. These may fundamentally change the way the company conducts its business and failure to meet objectives on time may lead to a catastrophic loss of business.

Some projects or programmes can be chaotic at times. Objectives are evolving and plans and priorities are constantly changing. There is a temptation to accept this chaos as a necessary 'nature of the beast'. However, it is essential to move the programme forward in a traditional project management way by making sure that objectives and plans move forward.

Once we have clear objectives and plans, programme managers must control two fundamental factors if they are to be successful:

• The business plan must be clearly identified,

• The implementation of the program must be made explicit.

This can be answered by isolating the fundamental cause of most, if not all major project problems. It can be argued that projects only fail due to two fundamental reasons:

• The plans are proven to be incorrect,

• The significance of these plans is misunderstood.

The capture, analysis, and communication of such assessments are, therefore, critical to the success of any project. This forms the basis of the Risk Management methodology. The Risk method has been applied by PsySys to help many diverse organisations to deliver large, complex projects and programmes on time, to budget and in meeting the expectations of demanding users.

3.2 METHODOLOGY

The focus of the methodology is based on he capture and analysis of the critical events and their assessments within the project plans, processes, and procedures.

The methodology is essentially a framework process that allows the capture of collective knowledge and viewpoints from those involved on the project, in a form that facilitates communication of events, assessments and ensures the pro-active management of risks. This is accomplished by dramatically improving communications, risks are avoided or managed to the optimum, and project objectives are delivered on time.

In essence, this is the mechanism by which the functions of programmes and projects are held together as a result of the principles operating within the *I.T. Risk Management* methodology:

The varied events, their assessments, and the consequential risks relating to or consisting of a system. Methodical in procedures and plans, these are addressed to those involved and deliberating within the parameters of their systems development responsibilities.

The results being dependable on interaction. The mutual or reciprocal action which encourages those involved in the programmes and projects to communicate with each other and to work closely with a view to solving the threatening events before they impact on the development of the system.

The individuals involved maintain a generic approach, which relates and characterises the whole group of those involved in assessing the events and attacking the threatening ones before they become risks to the development of the system. The end result being the avoidance of apparent problems within the pre-defined users' systems requirements.

This is enabled by following the methodology. The system architects and the risk management practitioners simply follow the approved body of systems development methods, rules and management procedures employed by their organisation. For practical or even ethical reasons, it must be noted that with such a philosophy, it is seldom possible to fulfil all requirements of very large organisational systems.

As such, the risk methodology is administered in applications. Putting to use such techniques and in applying the risk management principles in the development of various *applications* will involve numerous and varied activities. A concrete issue in developing new applications is the problem of communication among the people involved, the motivation constantly needed for *generic* work, the ability to *interact systematically* and in using a structured systems *methodology*.

3.3 RISK MANAGEMENT CYCLE

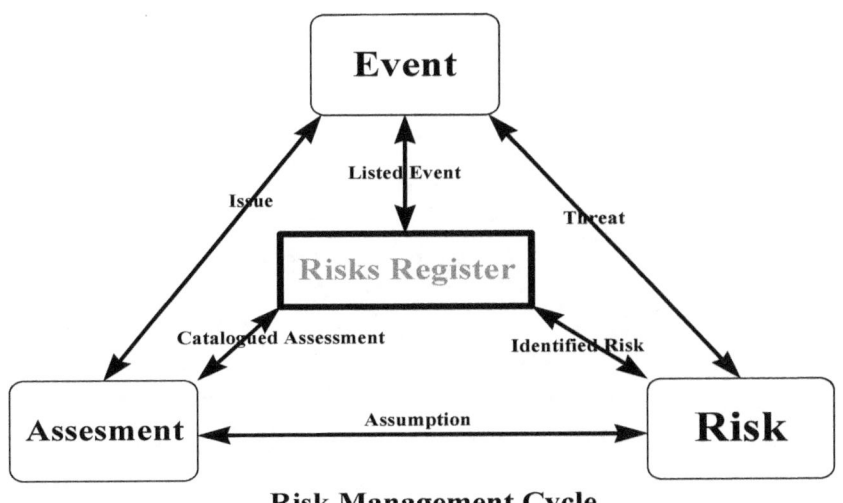

Risk Management Cycle

3.4 FEATURES AND BENEFITS APPROACH

The key features and benefits of the PsySys approach are:

☐ *Communication* — Provides a simple, common, language for the communication of risk up, down and sideways within the organisation, whilst avoiding the normal problems of political sensitivity and risk aversion.

☐ *Control* — Enhances project control by exception management and achieves an overview of risk at senior management levels.

☐ *Information* — Encourages the sharing of risk information, establishing common objectives, discouraging risk transfer and hence reducing the overall risk to all involved parties.

☐ *Flexible* — An adaptable process which is rigorously applied to ensure that all significant risks are identified and controlled at the appropriate time.

☐ *Acceptable* — The non-intrusive/non-bureaucratic management process improves management discipline across the organization and is readily accepted by project teams.

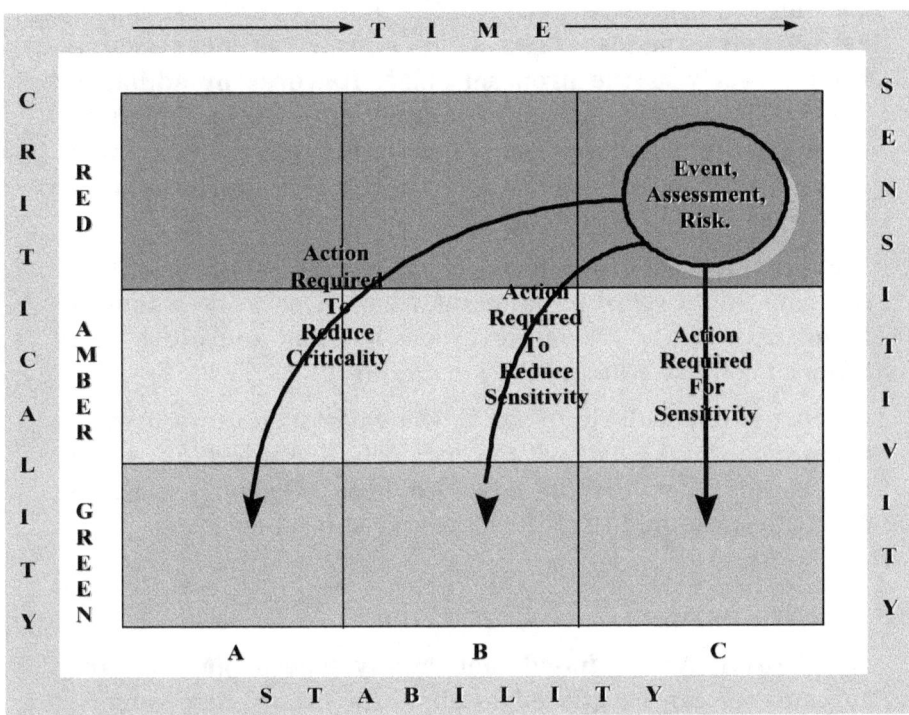

Project Criticality, Stability and Sensitivity: Measures To Be Taken To Reduce The Risk Impact

The core of *I.T. Risk Management* is the Assessment Analysis. This uses structured techniques to analyse project plans and identify the most sensitive events that are potentially unstable, and therefore the source of greatest risk.

Everything is rated on a GAR principle: Green, Amber and Red scale; where G is always 'good' and R is always 'bad'. This provides an instantly understood assessment on each stage: Events, Assessments, and Risks in relationship with the time scales as used in the plans. This, effectively, provides guidance on how best to attack the risk.

3.6 STRATEGIC COST ANALYSIS

Costing is a process within *I.T. Risk Management* that can be used to define the cost of risk within a project or business area from as early as the proposal stage. It works by adding a 'quality' dimension to the estimating process so that high quality estimates, based on relevant experience, are treated differently from low quality estimates which are little more than guesses.

The output takes the form of a probability distribution diagram and a set of assessments which need to be managed in order to move the curve to the left and squeeze it (i.e. reduce the likely cost and the uncertainty).

Costing is particularly useful in the early stages of a project when the final cost of the project is subject to great uncertainty. The process has also been effectively used to define business budgets for re-structured business areas.

3.7 RISK ADMINISTRATION SYSTEM TOOL

A Microsoft Access based tool or any type of an ordinary spreadsheet can be utilised to allow the events, assessments, and risks to be captured and reviewed by all stockholders in the program. In this way risks that would have been missed are captured through the identification of events.

3.8 WORK PLAN ANALYSIS

Work Plan Analysis is a set of techniques that enables a rapid risk assessment to be undertaken on a complex project which is already in progress.

It is always difficult to focus on the right areas when the project organisation is large and the plans are extensive and likely to be multi-levelled. Using Work Plan Analysis, the 'poor quality' areas of a project are quickly highlighted for further investigation.

One very successful application of this approach has been through the use of Project Readiness Assessment Walkthroughs. These are structured review meetings held just prior to major project milestones or deliverables. Initially the project team explain their self-evaluation of the project status and are questioned by an independent review team. Potential risks arising are captured using the Assessment Analysis process.

3.9 COMMUNICATING THE RISKS

The I.T. Risk Management techniques summarised above will only deliver its full benefits to any business if a suitable governance structure is quickly established to communicate the risk information and set suitable actions to mitigate the risks. The mapping of the process onto an organisation is the key step to ensuring that the investment in the *I.T. Risk Management* process is fully realised.

4 PRINCIPLES OF RISK MANAGEMENT

4.1 TEAM APPROACH

An enterprise must escape from a culture based on transfer of risk between parties, to a team approach that is focused on attacking the real source of the risks. Methods must be effective without the need for detailed, time consuming analysis.

4.2 DEFINITION OF A RISK

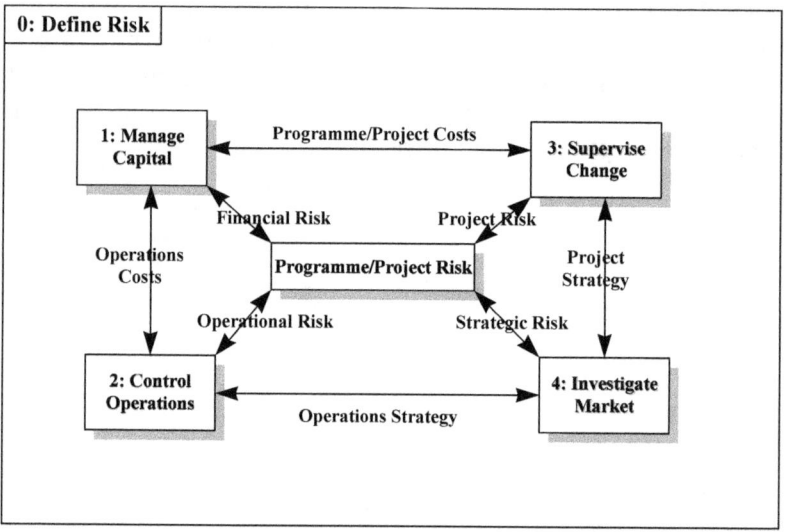

Programme/Project Risk: One Component Of The Total Business Risk.

A risk may be perceived as a possible loss. Risk is individual to a person or organisation because - what is perceived by one individual as a major risk may be perceived by another as a minor risk.

A risk is linked very strongly with competitiveness. Each decision has the possibility of resulting in loss. Each decision to introduce a new product into the marketplace can result in varying degrees of loss or gain. To be entrepreneurial is to accept risk, that is, the possibility of loss. A good entrepreneur's strength, however, is to make decisions which maximise possible gain. Hence minimise possible loss, which constitutes effective risk management.

Risk is inherent in all aspect of an organisation and may be viewed from four primary directions: financial, operational, programme/project and portfolio/products. Many risks are related to the running of the operations and its processes but is often in trying to change operations that the greatest risk is experienced. It is the management of risk in such 'change' projects that the I.T. Risk Management methodology addresses.

A project can be described in its simplest terms as: Planning to achieve specific objectives and then executing the plans. The emphasis is on the word 'plan' as without a plan we have no project. So in the context of a project, a risk is something which might disrupt the plans such that the objectives of the project are not met. The discipline of Project Risk Management is thus a framework of techniques which allows the project manager to pro-actively identify and manage risks before they develop into problems which will impact the project plans.

4.3 APPROACHES TO RISK MANAGEMENT

In recent years we have seen large projects in many areas of business suffering from a lack of control. The size of cost and time over-runs do not seem to be decreasing, despite the amount of management time which is being dedicated to analysing and quantifying the potential problems and selecting suitable personnel and processes. One may conclude that management, either do not have the correct methods and tools in place to attack the potential problems, or that they are not using, or do not understand, those which they do have.

In the early 1970's, the concepts of formal project risk management began to emerge. Hailed as the saviour of project managers, in practice the results have been mixed. Risk management has proved highly effective in certain mature industries - e.g. the Petrochemical or construction industry where project managers can base their estimates on years of similar engineering experience. Difficulties seem to be encountered when these traditional Risk Management methods are applied to innovative and fast evolving areas such as Information Technology.

4.4 EVENTS AND RISK REGISTERS

Most projects will have an Events Register and some may have what they call a Risk Register. In effect, this tends to be a list into which anyone can input their concerns. It will contain references to current problems, questions, and assessments, difficult activities about which there is reasonable confidence and the odd real risk.

In any large project the Events or Risk Register quickly becomes swamped with items that require very different actions and many which do not require any action at all. All this leads to an inevitable loss of focus. Further, the content tends to be biased towards current problems rather than future potential problems.

4.5 INDIVIDUAL INTERVIEWS

One-on-one interviews can be an effective way of capturing risks. When people are not inhibited by management and peers, they tend to be far more open about their concerns. Unfortunately, most use much unsophisticated approaches such as "what do you see as your risks?" or "what keeps you awake at night?" Thus, if the person interviewed is sensitive to discussing risks it may prevent the capture of any valuable information. At best the risks captured will tend to lack structure as they are not focused onto the future objectives that the project plans to achieve.

4.6 GROUP BRAINSTORMING

Group brainstorming can be a very effective technique for opening up a very complex situation. However, information can be subconsciously suppressed by peer pressure, which may bias the discussion on one area at the expense of the rest of the project. Inevitably the mass of information captured is often difficult to focus, prioritise, and allocate ownership.

In general, it should be remembered that the quality of the output is only as good as the quality of the input data.

4.7 RISK ANALYSIS AND QUANTIFICATION

Risks may be difficult to capture reliably and concisely but further problems are likely to be experienced when trying to analyse them. Virtually all approaches to risk analysis are based on estimating the factored impact of the risk. This exposure to risk is a combination of the chance (probability) of an event happening and the consequences (impact) if it does occur i.e.

Risk Exposure = Potential Impact x Probability of Occurrence

Fundamental problems arise when individuals are required to estimate, numerically, the impact and then predict (numerically) the probability. Estimates, which are often little more than guesses, result in a single point estimate of Risk Exposure, which is then given undeserved credibility in the detailed analysis of the risk and used as the basis for many major project decisions. Also, it is often the case that part of the risk impact can be quantified but often not the major part. An example can be based on an attempt to quantify bad publicity, quality, and relationship.

Some processes add complexity by rating the impact of risks in terms of financial, time scales, quality, performance etc., which quickly become very tedious to maintain.

4.8 RISK CONTROL AND FOLLOW-THROUGH

Many risk management systems fail due to a lack of follow-through on actions. There is a surprising tendency to identify risks and then watch them happen!

This is caused by:

☐ Failure to use the risk register to set appropriate action plans,

☐ Lack of regular updates/maintenance of the risk register,

☐ Absence of named owners and deadlines (lack of ownership),

☐ Tracking generalities rather than specifics,

☐ Concentrating on what can be done if the risk occurs rather than stopping the risk happening (pro-active),

☐ Trying to transfer the risk elsewhere, without considering the consequences.

4.9 RISK TRANSFER

Risk transfer often occurs because the partner who knows most about the level of risk within the enterprise (i.e. the supplier/purchaser relationship) is encouraged to transfer this to the other partner. Once accomplished, the party with the most knowledge of the risk relaxes and the most ignorant partner inherits the risk. An example of this is the Purchaser insisting on a fixed-price contract in a poorly defined contract when they know that the supplier does not understand the scope of the contract.

The supplier then has a tendency to deliver the minimum possible and obtain sign-off for everything, irrespective of quality. The effect of this type of commercial 'table-tennis' is actually to increase the level of risk within the enterprise as the real risks pile up without intervention.

What is needed is a method that identifies and encourages the attack of real risk at source. Such a method would force projects within the enterprise to become pro-active by attacking risks, rather than waiting for events to unfold and then counting the cost, as recorded in the previous month's financial returns.

4.10 RISK AND PROJECT MANAGEMENT

There is often a tendency to treat risk management as no more than another necessary evil of project management. Thus, it often becomes an additional administrative burden for the Project Manager and consequently does not get the quality attention to make it work effectively.

In order to make risk management work, a shift in philosophy is required. This must lead the project team to view the process not just as another component of project management, but more as the communication stabiliser that holds the project together.

5. PRINCIPLES OF RISK METHODOLOGY

5.1 PROCESS

The *I.T. Risk Management* method described in this book aims to provide an effective means of managing risks within all types of projects. The *I.T. Risk Management* process grew out of a thorough assessment of the problems often encountered in project management and the techniques of the traditional risk management approaches that have been used to try and improve the situation.

Both good and bad principles were noted and new techniques were introduced to address key deficiencies. The resulting *I.T. Risk Management* process has a proven track record of delivering tangible results in large projects across a diverse range of organisations.

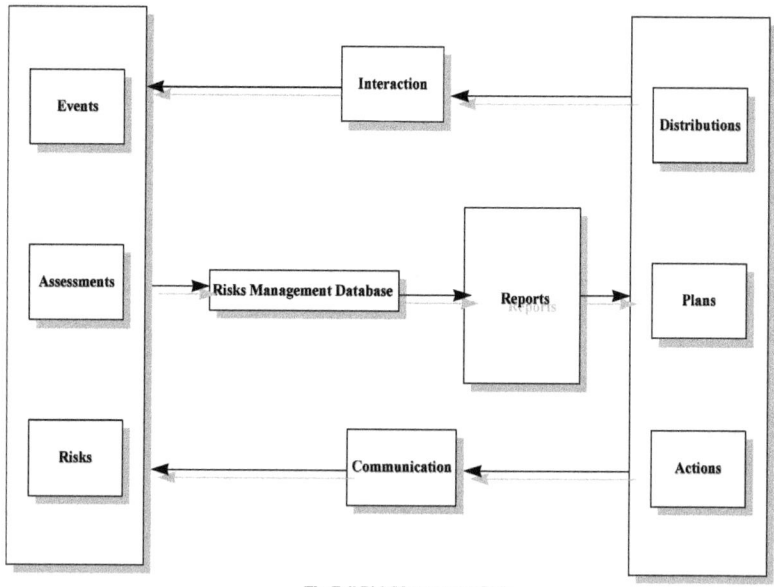

The Full Risk Management Cycle

5.2 COMMUNICATION OF ASSESSMENTS

As already highlighted, a fundamental reason for project failure is the lack of quality communications both within the project and between the programme and its environment. Most problems incurred by projects could be avoided if information was effectively communicated in a timely fashion. The problem is that there is so much information that it is difficult to decide what needs to be communicated and to who. This is where assessments come in.

Everything important associated with a project can be captured and tracked as an assessment:

☐ Activities are sized on the basis of assessments,

☐ Milestones are set according to assessments,

☐ Dependencies are based on assessments,

☐ Plans are executed by making assessments.

Therefore, the capture, analysis, and communication of assessments are critical to the success of any project, and this forms the core of the I.T. Risk Management and the Project Management process.

5.3 CURRENT PROJECT PLAN - BASELINE

Risks are identified by capturing the critical assessments in the project plans are uncertain. In other words, whatever might stop the objectives, timescales, and budget of the project plan being achieved. In this way, all assessments are effectively referenced to the project plans. Consequently, the plan provides the focus for the risk management process.

This approach keeps the risks specific, forward looking and ensures that the plan is always sufficiently detailed and up to date.

5.4 UNCERTAINTY EQUALS RISK

Risk is inherent whenever there is uncertainty. The best judges of uncertainty are those who are asked to make estimates for the plans and, in most circumstances, the people who will actually have to do the work make the best estimators.

Combining this principle with the assessments captured from the project plans leads us to rate assessments for quality/uncertainty. Analysis is concentrated onto the areas of the project about which little is known and particularly the inter-dependencies that often represent the highest risk.

5.5 QUALITY JUDGEMENT SCALE

To capture this vital information about how sure the estimator is, each estimator is asked, not only for assessments or the value of any estimate, but also, what quality he or she considers the assessment or estimate to be. This is not a judgement of the skill of the estimator. It is a self-assessment of the current quality of the basic information, upon which the project plans are based.

The risks scale is defined for multiple uses throughout the process. It always means effectively the same thing i.e. A is

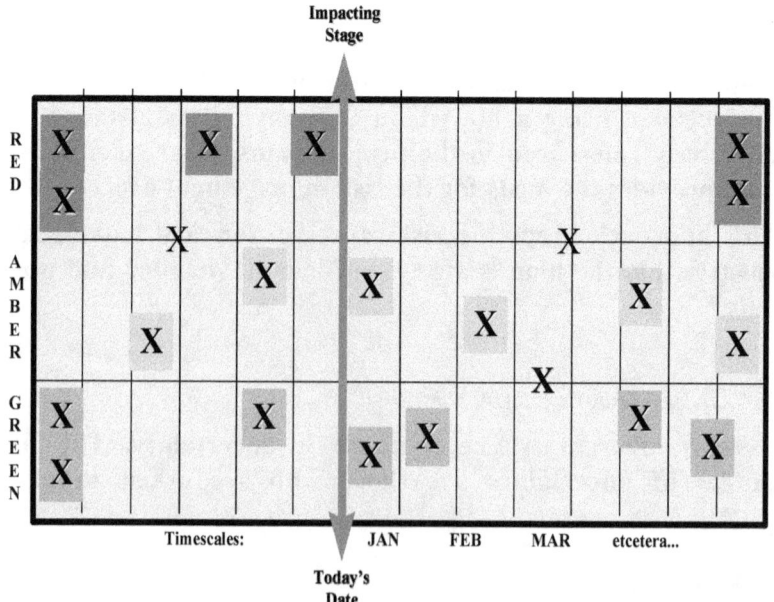

Impacting Risks

always good and C is always bad. B expresses tendencies to the two extremes.

☐ A (Green) means very good, high confidence, not important

☐ B (Amber) means fairly good, reasonable confidence, not very important

☐ C (Red) means very poor, little or no confidence, and

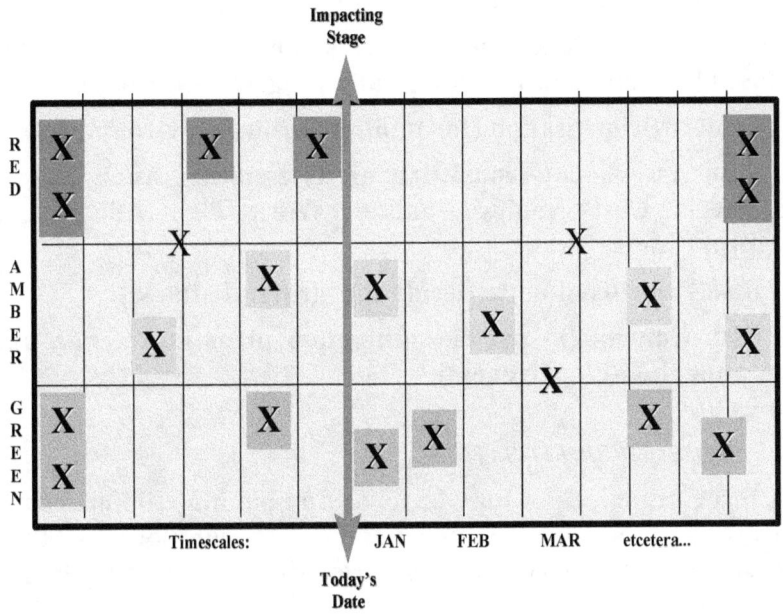

Impacting RIsks

critically important.

It should be noted that the method does not allow the estimator to say that the estimate or assessment is of average quality. The whole principle is that we should be forced to make a choice between good, high confidence and bad, low confidence estimates and cannot 'sit on the fence'.

Using these simple A, B, C terms to express degrees of uncertainty, it is possible to encourage the estimator to reveal a wide range of uncertainty. Also, it is often possible to persuade him or her to make estimates when not normally prepared to do so. Being able to qualify an assessment or estimate with a C quality, often assures the estimators that they will not be forced into a given value or statement. We can thus gain vital information about the uncertainty and therefore the risks that may lie at the heart of the project without even asking for a risk.

5.6 PROCESS OVERVIEW

The *I.T. Risk Management* process consists of an integrated closed loop method, which logically progresses through:

☐ Project Prioritisation (for multiple project environments),

☐ Risk Assessment (consisting of Assessments Analysis plus Strategic Cost Analysis and/or Work Plan Analysis, if appropriate),

☐ Risk Prioritisation (to decide the 'order of attack'),

☐ Risk Control (to put the mitigation plans into action and monitor their effectiveness).

12.2.2

5.7 PROJECT PRIORITISATION

A large organisation may have, at any one time, hundreds of projects of varying size, and nature. Yet many organisations have no formal mechanism for prioritising projects leading to problems such as:

☐ Not knowing which projects should be approved/resourced,

☐ Uncertainty as to which projects should be formally assessed for risk.

Once the critical and potentially risky projects have been identified, I.T. Risk Management offers three risk assessment techniques to identify and analyse the specific risks within each project.

The Assumption Analysis technique provides a backbone onto which the Strategic Cost Analysis and/or Work Plan Analysis approaches can be built.

In this respect Assumption Analysis would always be applied, Strategic Cost Analysis would be used in the early stages of a project or proposal to address the uncertainty in the cost/pricing of the project and Work Plan Analysis may be used to assess a very complex project which is well progressed.

5.8 RISK PRIORITISATION

The specific risks captured from each project risk assessment needs to be prioritised in order to allocate resources and decide the order in which the risks should be addressed.

The method provides a simple framework which rates each risk for Criticality, Controllability, and Impact Timing. The resulting list of risks is captured in a Microsoft Access Risk Register (or any type of spreadsheet) and the risks are summarised in a diagram which provides an executive overview of the project risk profile.

The diagram shown in *8.5* can also be used in this stage, as this can be modified to include the list of impacting risks as reported by the Risk Register. Although this figure shows risks with the letter X, in reality, the Xs can be replaced by the actual system generated risks reports.

5.9 RISK CONTROL

This provides a framework for risk control based on taking both strategic and tactical views of attacking risks. The strategic approach is achieved by applying trend analysis to the underlying assessments to identify any strong Risk Drivers, which can be neutralised together.

Tactical approaches match the complexity of the risk action plan to the complexity of the risk to minimise bureaucracy for simple-to-manage risks, whilst maintaining the necessary formality for complex risks.

The purpose of the diagram below is to show to the reader that at a certain point of time, measures have to be taken to reduce the impact of a Critical, Unstable and/or a Sensitive event, assessment and/or risk.

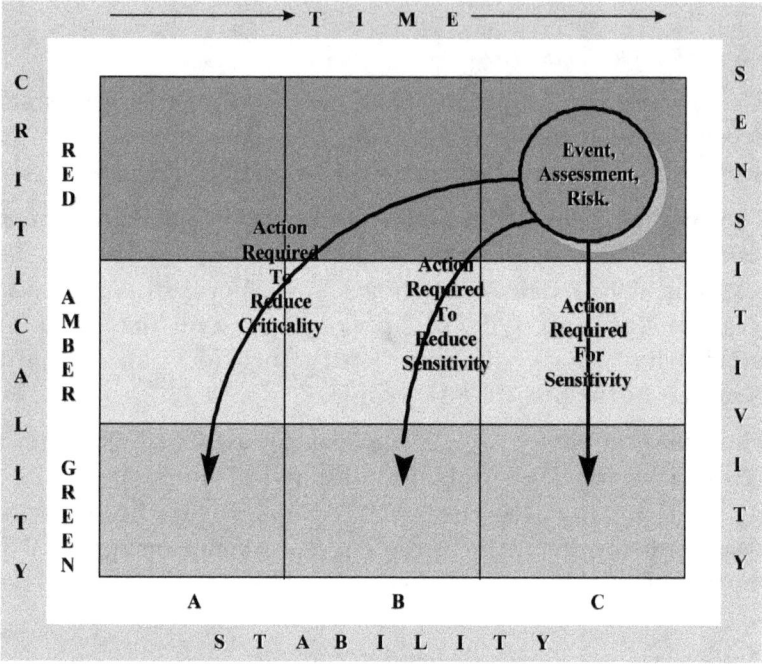

Project Criticality, Stability and Sensitivity: Measures To Be Taken To Reduce The Risk Impact

6.1 RE-PLANNING

The key aspect of a project in trouble is that it requires re-planning to put it back on track. Thus, the timing of the risk assessment relative to this planning process is very important.

If the re-planning process has not started there will be very little of the new approach to assess. It may be possible to influence this new approach by undertaking a risk assessment of the options being considered. To do this an Assumption Analysis of the alternative high-level plans can provide a useful framework for decision making.

If the project has been re-planned, then an Assessment Analysis of the new plans, possibly supplemented by Work Plan Analysis, is an appropriate way forward.

6.2 INTERVIEWS WITH KEY PEOPLE

Identifying the right people to interview is critical to producing a comprehensive and coherent picture of the risks facing a project. So, to decide on who should be interviewed, start with the project or programme organisational structure.

Depending on the scope of the risk assessment (i.e. single project, programme of multiple projects, portfolio of business projects etc.) it may be necessary to map the organisational hierarchy to ensure that the right people are interviewed and that the risks arising are reviewed at an appropriate level.

Working with the Programme or Project Manager, try to identify the 'key players'. A key player is someone within the programme/project who is likely to have either specific expertise in a particular area and/or insight into the environment in which the project is being implemented.

Key players tend to be Project Managers for a programme or Team Managers for a project with the addition of Users involved in the requirement capture and other activities. This group would likely form the initial interview list.

During the interview, these people should decide who else they need to participate. Interviewers need to exercise their judgement when evaluating the responses to this question. Typically it is necessary to go down at least one level below the Project/Team manager unless the team size is small.

One of the key features of the I.T. Risk Management process is that of obtaining counter viewpoints within the organisation. Thus, the more people that are interviewed, the better. However, if many projects are being assessed for risk within an organisation, resource constraints will inevitably lead to reducing the interview pool. Under these circumstances at least two counter viewpoints must be obtained within each project. (e.g.: business manager and technical manager) so that the assessment ratings can be compared.

6.3 CHOOSING RISK ASSESSMENT TEAM

The team that will operate and manage the I.T. Risk Management process requires a particular set of skills and background to be successful:

☐ Experience of working in large (preferably non-consulting) projects and managing (preferably) medium sized projects (say 10-20 people).

☐ Understanding of project planning principles and some exposure to associated tools.

☐ Forceful personalities to ensure quality data captures in difficult client situations.

☐ IT background, in order to understand the issues in IT projects and to help with using the I.T. Risk Management support tools.

☐ Some understanding of the clients business.

Note that it can sometimes be a disadvantage to have too much knowledge of the clients business in applying the I.T. Risk Management process. This is because there may be a tendency for the interviewer to get into too much detail in non-risky areas and take too much of the client's time in the process.

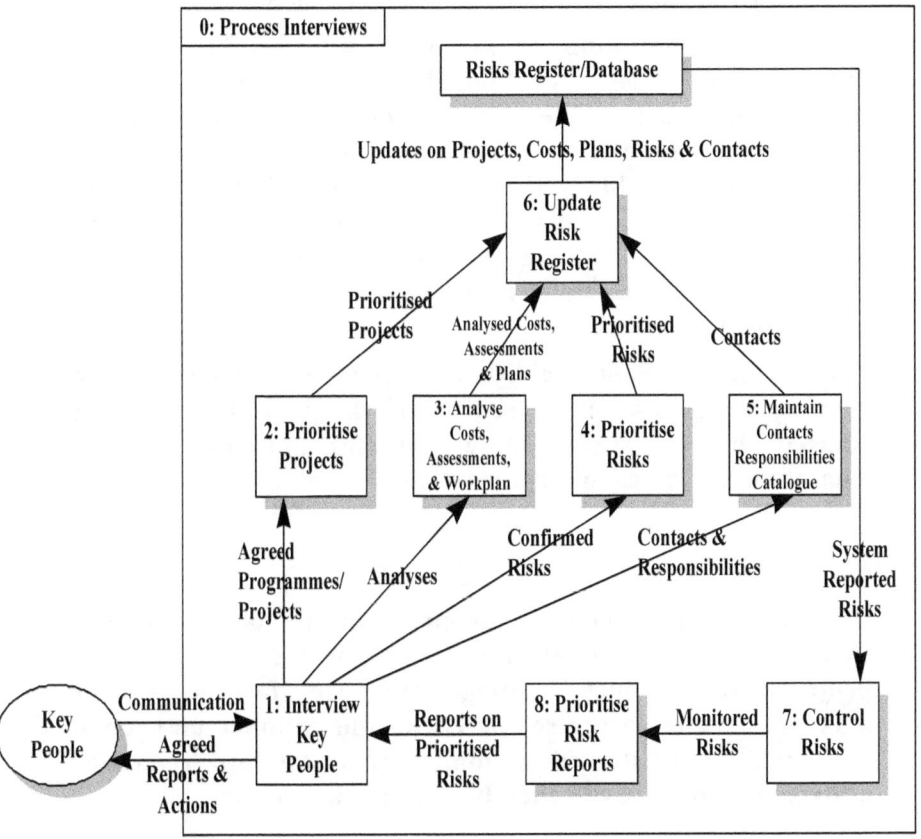

The Interviewing Process

6.4 RISK REVIEW MEETINGS

After the initial round of interviews, a suitable forum must be established to discuss the risks identified. The client may suggest that the risks are discussed as part of the regular project meeting. This should be resisted unless the risks are an early agenda item and there will be sufficient time to get through the agenda with this additional discussion.

Typically, a minimum of an hour will be required for discussion of the risks - all if possible but just the most critical if not. If discussion of the risks is left to the end there will often be little time (or concentration) left to do the process justice. Also, it is likely that some events will end up being discussed twice. If discussed first, the risks tend to focus the meeting and get away from talking about progress onto the things that need to be discussed - i.e. what threatens the success of the project.

The best method is to establish a specific Risk Review Meeting with a representation consisting of the Risk Owners and chaired by the Programme Director, or the process 'champion' in the client organisation.

6.5 PROJECT PRIORITISATION PROCESS

In order to help refine the appropriate positioning of projects, each business area must identify two or three current key projects with which management are familiar. After agreement between the senior client and supplier managers, these will be positioned to make up a standard reference matrix. This matrix will then be used as the baseline.

6.6 POSITIONING NEW PROJECTS

Initial positioning of the new project should be undertaken by the supplier and client project managers, together, as early as possible in the project. Complete consensus is not always possible at this stage, due to incomplete understanding of the business and technical issues involved.

However, it is essential that consensus is reached before any approval boards, or it is clear that the project is not ready to proceed. Lack of consensus can result in biased project ratings. Too high a rating will waste resources and cause frustration within the project team due to excessive management attention. Too low a rating will result in management neglect and consequently, increased risk.

6.7 PROJECT APPROVAL AND RESOURCES

In practice, the primary factor that is taken into consideration when approving a project is the Business Criticality. There are many projects that could be undertaken and only a finite resource pool available, so only the projects that will most improve the organisation's business should be approved.

Once management endorsement has been obtained, the results of the positioning exercise should be published to the teams and senior management.

6.8 PROJECTS CHANGE ON DIAGRAM

Once a project has been positioned it will be subject to review at least once every phase and certainly before progressing to the next stage. The most significant event in the life of a project is likely to be if it moves within either matrix.

A project may move because it is discovered that it is more or less complex than previously thought. It may have grown or been reduced in size. It may have become more or less critical to the client's business.

If a project moves, it is indicating something about the management approach required in the future. In particular, the approach to risk management should be reviewed and projects moving towards the top-right corner of the matrix should be assessed whilst projects moving towards the bottom left corner may be dropped from the risk assessment process.

6.9 RISK MANAGEMENT DECISION

The position of a project on the diagram is also used to determine which projects should be assessed formally for risk going forward. The threshold can be set at any appropriate level. For example, some organisations work on the principle that any project judged to be a C, on either matrix, should be assessed for risk using the I.T. Risk Management process. Projects falling below this threshold are still encouraged to use a formal method for risk assessment, but it is not mandated.

6.10 RISK IDENTIFICATION AND ANALYSIS

The risk method uses three windows; Assessment Analysis, Strategic Cost Analysis and Work Plan Analysis, to obtain a clear view of the source of any risk.

Although it is possible to create risk by poor planning and management, an element of risk is inherent in any enterprise. The main problem is to find a method of identifying the sources of the risks in time to allow specific actions to be taken to avoid or reduce the impact.

The nature of the project risks varies with the nature of the tasks, the size and the development phase of the project. Later phases may make use of methods for identifying risk based on the project's experiences to date. In early phases, good quality information and experience is scarce. Thus, different phases and different types of risk are best looked at by using different techniques and tools.

By using all these windows over the life of a project we increase our chances of identifying the major risks which lie within the project and to understand the nature of each risk.

The process ultimately allows us to represent each risk in terms of:

☐ The potential criticality of the risk in terms of impact on the core project objectives,

☐ The point in time that the risk will impact the project if unresolved,

☐ The likelihood of the risk occurring.

Using these three analysis techniques; Strategic Cost Analysis, Assessment Analysis and Work Plan Analysis, it is possible to generate a single list that contains all the fundamental risks to the project. This list can then be used to decide which elements represent important risks and should thus be subject to proactive Risk Management by the creation and execution of dedicated Risk Plans.

7 COMMUNICATING RISKS

7.1 PRESENTATION

Communicating risks to senior management groups is always difficult as they are often not familiar with the detail of the project. Subsequently, the risks need to be presented in a concise, clear way which explains what is causing the risk (and therefore indicates what needs to be done) and what would be the consequences if the risk is allowed to impact the project.

Thus assessments are converted into risks using the form:

If (the assessment proves incorrect),

Then (describe the consequences to the project or business).

It is important to express the full consequences of the risk or it may fail the "so-what", test when submitted to senior management. A good principle is to describe at least the immediate impact and the ultimate impact on the project programme or business.

An alternative representation of a risk is to leave the assessments stated in the positive and add the impact. The advantage of this is that the risk can still be expressed in a positive sense. Some people find this very important.

7.2 CATEGORISATION OF ASSESSMENTS

When capturing assessments, it is often useful to identify what is driving the Sensitivity and Stability ratings allocated to it so that the source (or "driver" of the risk) is clear. This is simply achieved by categorising assessments into one of three types:

☐ Policy where the assessment relates to a business decision or policy, standards, resourcing priorities etc. The assessment requires management intervention to bring it under control.

☐ Milestone where the timescales of the activities are being 'squeezed' or timescale dependencies on other projects, suppliers etc. The assessment would be no problem if more time were available.

☐ Technical where the complexity of the undertaking is driving the ratings (e.g. untried design, hardware and software constraints, complex organisations etc.). The complexity is such that mistakes are likely irrespective of the time available.

Categorising assessments in this way can make the selection of appropriate Risk Plans easier by ensuring that the true source of the risk is addressed. Further, it can allow a strategic view of the risks to be obtained but only when a statistically large number of risks are being tracked.

7.3 PROJECT READINESS WALKTHROUGHS

Project Readiness Walkthroughs are a highly effective way of ensuring that all risks have been captured from the assessments analysis process. When used independently from, or prior to, an Assessments Analysis, the walkthrough provides a start to the risk assessment process which is particularly useful when time is short.

Project walkthrough:

☐ Assess the readiness to meet milestones for high-priority projects,

☐ Identify any corporate resource contention that may exist, and assist with prioritisation,

☐ Identify common events and risks, and communicate information to support other project teams,

☐ Help project teams achieve their goals by identifying and/or providing resources for assistance as needed,

☐ Assess enterprise-wide risk through the evaluation of multiple projects.

The walkthrough is completed by going through the As and Bs and asking for them to be (briefly) justified. Any additional assessments or risks are logged.

The matrix is updated to reflect the risks identified to produce an exit matrix.

The risks reviewed regularly and actions stated to ensure that they are brought under control.

7.4 ASSESSMENTS AND RISKS REGISTER

All assessments captured should be held in an Assessments Register. Only critical assessments will be converted into risks and held in a Risk Register. This is done by filtering the assessments and consolidating them into risks. All information captured will be rationalised and details of their source and consequences will be traceable.

7.5 POSITIONING RISKS

In certain instances the risk may undermine the basic objectives of the project and no amount of money will save the project if such a risk impacts. If not resolved, the uncertainty may halt the progress of the project. Such a risk may be related to the overall programme, a part of the programme, an individual part of the design, or even a particular module of software. This, also, provides a way of representing the effect of such risks on the overall project, where cost impact is small or meaningless.

The timing of a risk should always equate to the latest time to start the first necessary action. In this respect, it is analogous with trying to stop a cancer. This must be done at the point that it starts to grow, not when it can be first being seen.

7.6 RISK REGISTER REPORTS

Impact Diagrams provide an overview or risk profile of the project. However, the detail of the risks is required for the risk review meeting in order that the detail of the risks can be seen, discussed and actions taken.

The order of the risks in the report is important so that senior management can focus on the key risks first.

If the impact diagram is used to prioritise the risk register the time element can be easily included. For instance there may be an urgent AMBER criticality, C controllability risk that needs attention that is not an obvious priority if the Risk Report is prioritised by Criticality and Controllability alone.

In essence the easiest way to prioritise is to use the Impact Diagram and to treat the highest priority risk as the one nearest to the origin, the next nearest being number two and so on. The intention is to order the risks so that they are roughly in the right order.

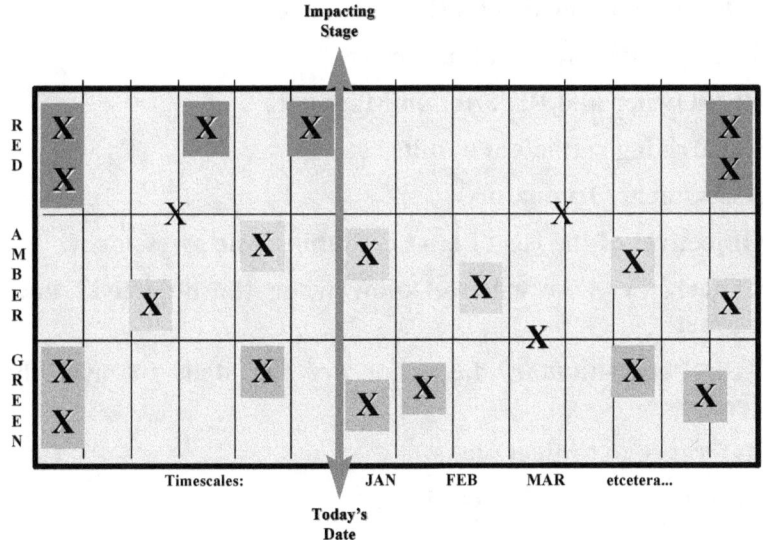

Impacting Risks

7.7 RISK PLANS REQUIREMENTS

Risks which cannot be resolved by improved planning must be tackled individually through the use of dedicated Risk Plans. Ultimately, the plans for reducing the risks must be incorporated into the main project plans.

Risk Plans may be divided into "Simple" or "Complex", irrespective of the potential impact of the risk. Simple means that it is possible to resolve the risk quickly say by a simple phone call or single task. For such risks, monitoring the status on the Risk Report is sufficient and minimises bureaucracy. Complex risks require significant resources and time to resolve them and for these a formal Risk Plan is required.

7.8 COMPONENTS OF A FORMAL RISK PLAN

For complex risks, it is essential that a structured plan is formulated. This will clarify thinking, provide the necessary visibility, and feed directly into the main planning process:

The basic components of a Risk Plan are:

☐ The risk statement and its ratings,

☐ Risk Owner and Risk Action Manager,

☐ The driving statement and its ratings,

☐ Assessment Originator,

☐ Objectives of the Risk Plan i.e. Stabilise the assessment,

☐ Criteria i.e. how will we know when the objectives have been met,

☐ Risk Plan summary i.e. what are the steps to meet the objectives,

☐ Reference to project plans,

☐ Additional resources required,

☐ Monitoring process i.e. how often and by whom,

☐ Re-assessment of the driving assessment (completed after execution of the Risk Plan)

☐ Fall-back plans i.e. what we do if the Risk Plan fails.

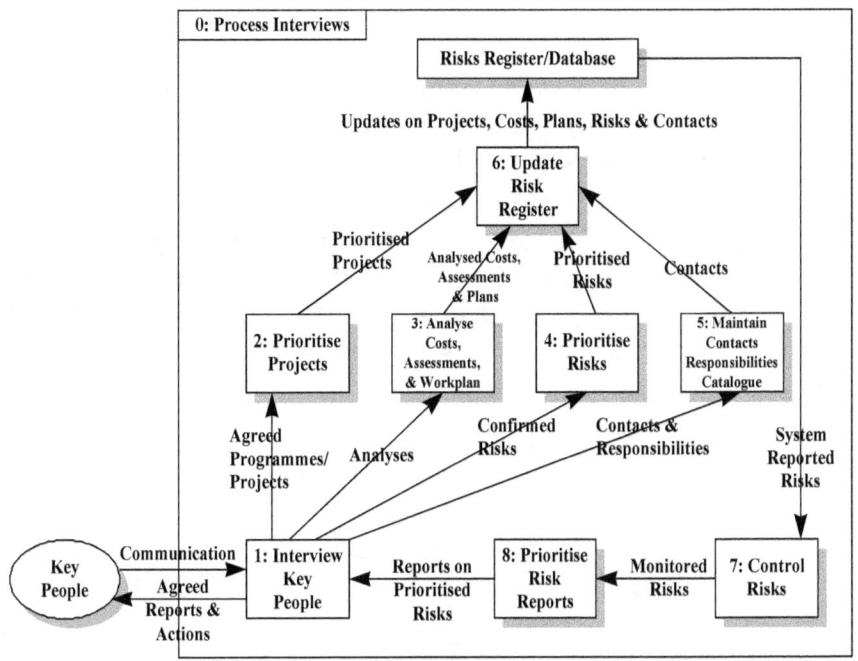

The Interviewing Process

8 METHODOLOGIES

8.1 INTEGRATING METHODOLOGIES

In handing over and in applying any Risk Management method, as in any other Management tool, the integration of all existing methodologies is of primary importance.

In choosing the new owner of the I.T. Risk Management methodology, consideration must be given regarding the experience possessed by the new proprietor. Preference should be given to the people with systems methodology and management procedures training and experience.

The diagram below will serve as a guide on what the knowledge should include.

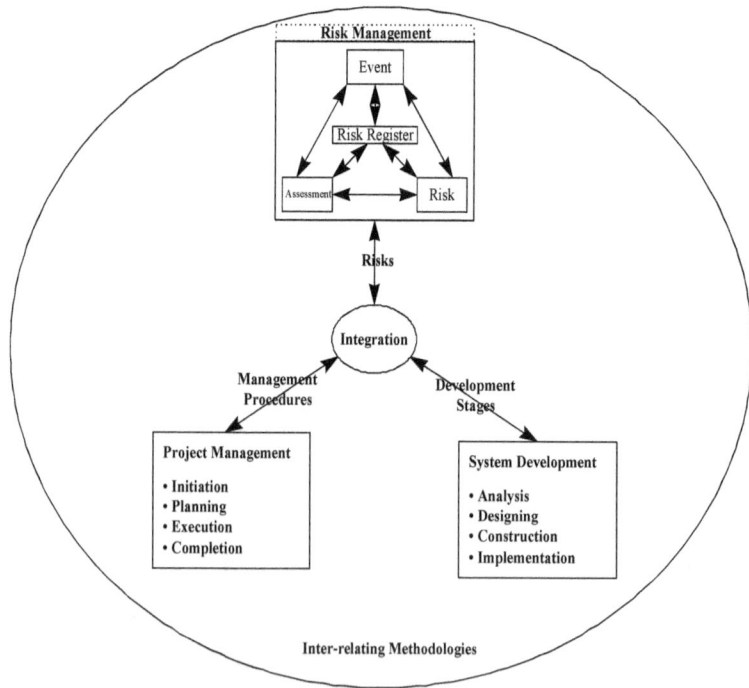

8.2 Integration

The diagrammatic flow shown below is the desired overall integration of related top-level processes:

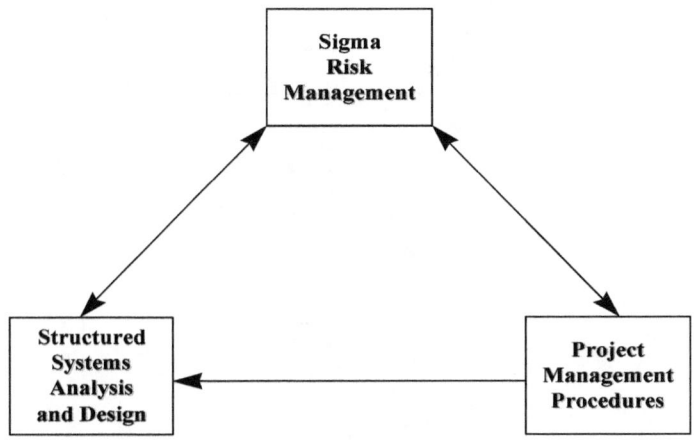

Integration Of Methodologies

8.3 SUGGESTED INTERFACING

The suggested interfacing of the Structured Systems Analysis and Design methodology and the Project Management procedures to the Risk Management processes may be done separately as shown in the diagram below:

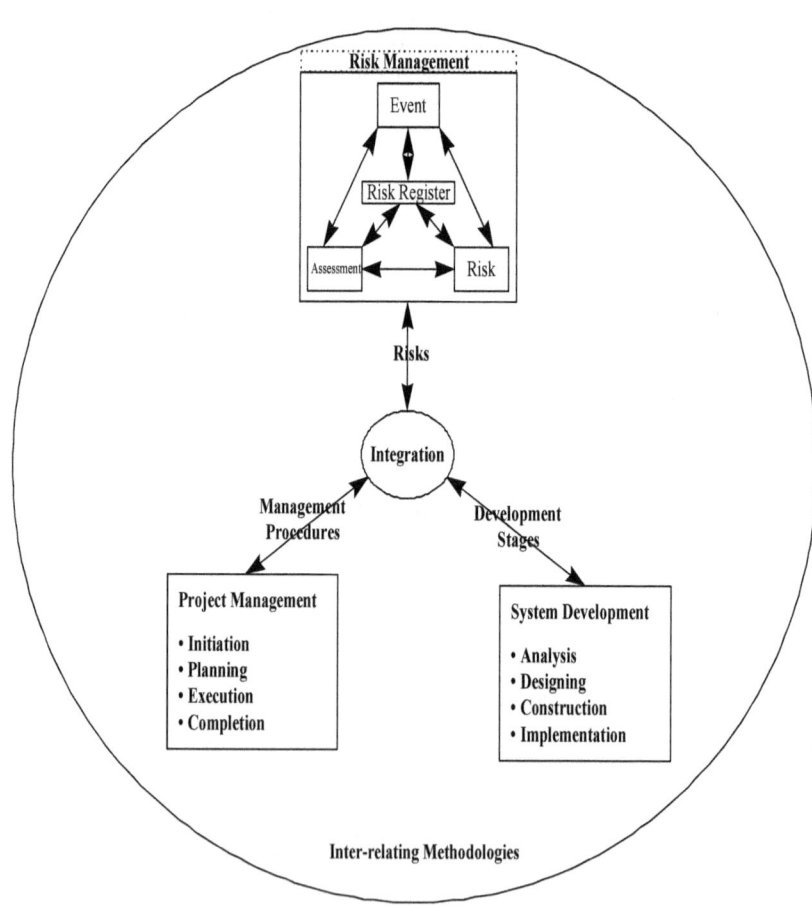

9. MANAGING THE RISK PROGRAMME

9.1 DIAGRAMMATIC REPRESENTATION

The term *'Sigma'* used in the process boxes in some diagrams below is based on the P*sySys* method of Risk Management.

9.2   RISK MANAGEMENT DECOMPOSITION

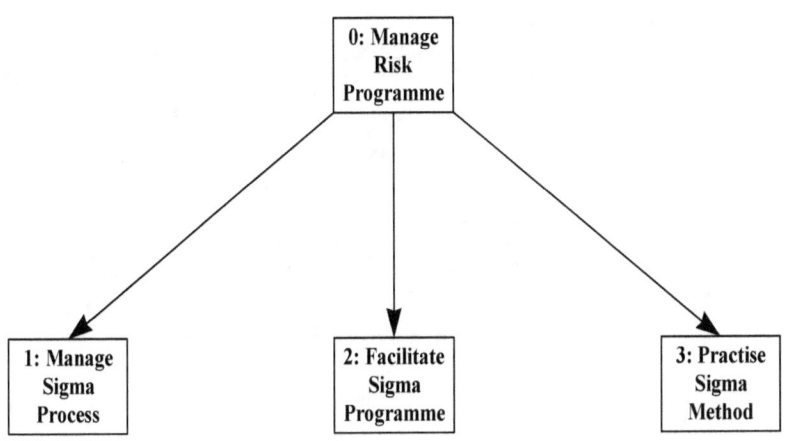

The Sigma Risk Management Decomposition

9.3 RISK PROGRAMME MANAGEMENT

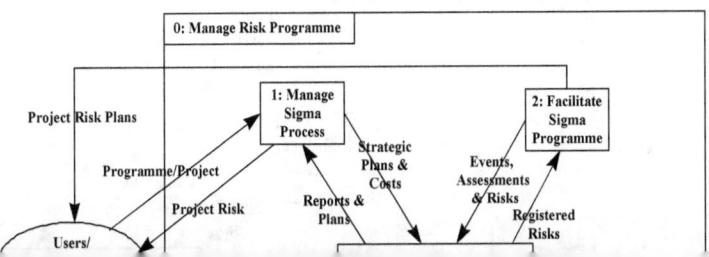

9.4 *MANAGING THE RISK PROCESS*

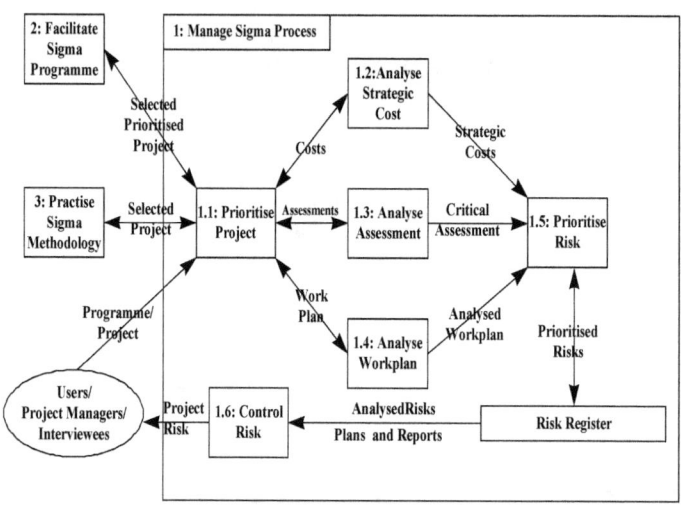

9.5 *FACILITATION OF RISK PROGRAMME*

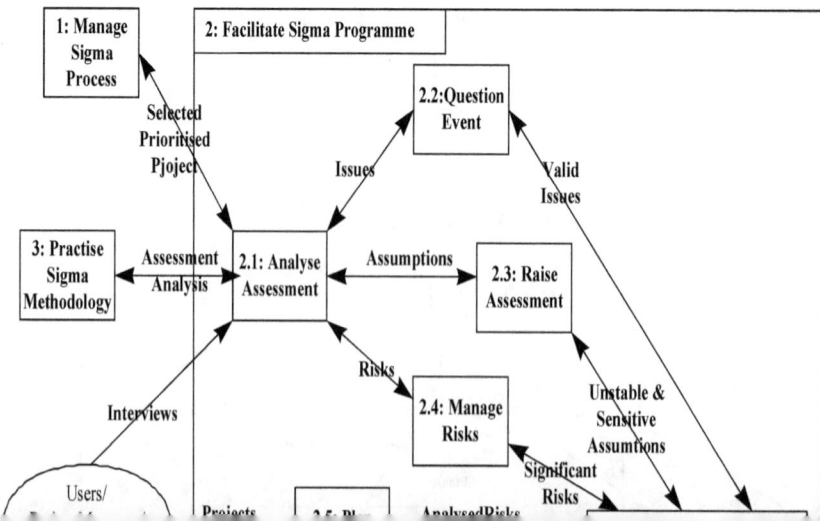

9.6 PRACTISING RISK METHODOLOGY

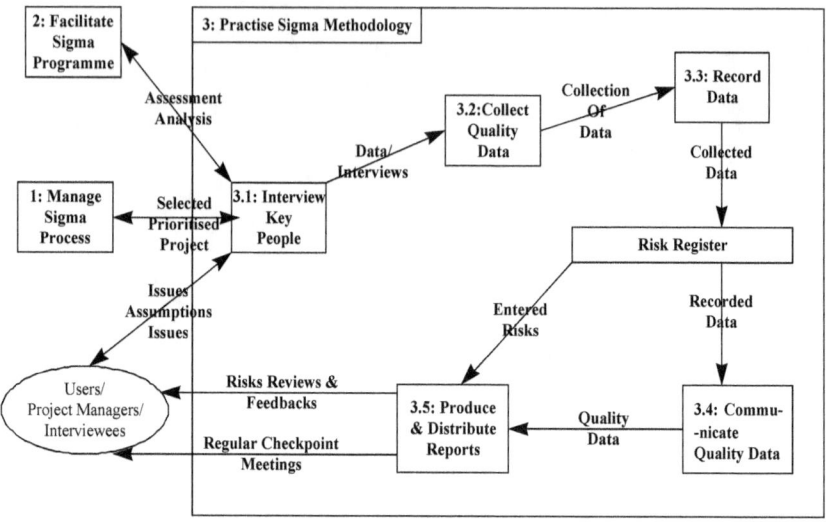

9.7 DATAFLOW DIAGRAMS RELATIONSHIP

All dataflow diagrams shown in above pages are based on the PsySys Limited manuals and handouts as used for the Risk Management training.

DATAFLOW DIAGRAMS:	DESCRIPTION OF DIAGRAMS AND THEIR PROCESSES.
0: Manage Risk Programme	Project: something complex that you want (plan) to happen.
	Risk: Something that you don't want to happen.
	Project management: Planning and making things happen.
	Risk management: Attacking anything that

	might disturb the plans
1: Manage I.T. Risk Management Process	The Risk Management process consists of an integrated closed loop method which logically progresses through: • Project Prioritisation, • Strategic Cost Analysis, • Assessment Analysis, • Work Plan Analysis, • Risk Prioritisation, • Risk Control.
1.1 Prioritise Project	Only complex and critical projects need to have a fully structured risk management process in place.
1.2 Analyse Strategic Cost	Strategic Cost Analysis provides a means of assessing the cost risk in a project in its very early stages and "kick-starts" the risk management process.
1.3 Analyse Assessment	Fundamentally, projects only fail due to two reasons either the wrong assumptions were made or the significance of the assumptions was not understood.
1.4 Analyse Work plan	Work Plan Analysis may be used to focus on the risky areas of detailed, multi-level project plans when time is of the essence.
1.5 Prioritise Risk	Prioritisation allows the Project Manager to divert limited resources at the most critical project risk.
1.6 Control Risk	Risks may be attacked at both the strategic and tactical levels. Strategic approaches look for trends and underlying causes for groups of risks. Tactical approaches take each risk at

	face value.
2: Facilitate Programme	The Risk Management Programme is essentially a framework process that allows the capture of collective knowledge and viewpoints from those involved on the project, in a form that facilitates communication of events, assessments and ensures pro-active management of risks. By dramatically improving communication, risks are avoided or managed proactively and project objectives are delivered on time.
2.1: Analyse Assessment	The core of the Risk Management is the Assessment Analysis. This uses structured techniques to analyse project plans and identify the most sensitive assumptions that are potentially unstable, and therefore the source of greatest risk.
2.2: Question Event	Events are open questions which are holding up plans/implementation. An Event is any open question which has been asked at the right time to which a high quality answer cannot be provided without escalation.
2.3: Raise Assessment	Many Events are closed by making Assessments in plans. An Assessment is a single, simple, positive, or negative statement.
2.4: Manage Risks	Unstable/sensitive assumptions create risks. Significant risks need to be managed formally. Definition: A Risk is a simple statement of the form: "IF" Assumption proves incorrect, "THEN"

	Describe the impact.
2.5: Plan Risks	Risk Plans impact project plans.
	Events, Assessments, and risks are inherent in the project plans.
	Population of assessment and risks registers by progressing Risk Plans/Main/Project Plans.
3: Practise Risk Methodology	The Role of a Risk Management Practitioner includes:
	Interview 'Key People' within the project,
	To collect 'Quality' data,
	Ensure the data collected is recorded in the Risk Register,
	Communicate the 'Quality' data to Project staff,
	Produces accurate and timely reports for meetings:
	Weekly Check Point Meetings,
	Risk Review Boards.
3.1: Interview Key People	Identifying the right people to interview is critical to producing a comprehensive and coherent picture of the risks facing a project. So, to decide who should be interviewed, start with the project or programme organisational structure. Depending on the scope of the risk assessment it may be necessary to map the organisational hierarchy to ensure that the right people are interviewed and that the risks arising are reviewed at an appropriate level.
3.2: Collect Quality Data	This function requires to:
	Interview 'Key People' within the project,

	Collect 'Quality' data.
3.3: Record Data	Having Interviewed the 'Key People' within the project and collected the 'Quality' data: Ensure the data collected is recorded in the Risk Register.
3.4: Communicate Quality Data	The interviews of 'Key People' within the project have been completed, the 'Quality' data recorded in the Risk Register and communicated to Project staff, the next function is: Facilitate and ensure the Risk Management process stays on track.
3.5: Produce Reports	After the initial round of interviews, a suitable forum must be established to discuss the risks identified. The best method is to establish a specific Risk Review Meeting with a representation consisting of the Risk Owners and chaired by the Programme Director or the process 'champion' in the client organisation. The main function is to: • Produce accurate and timely reports for meetings, • Weekly Check Point Meetings, • Risk Review Boards.

Detester/Database Of Events, Assessments, and Risks Register Description.

Data Store: *Risk* *Register*	All events, assessments, and risks captured should be held in a Risks Register. Remember, only critical assessments will be converted into risks and held in a Risk Register. Thus, by filtering the assessments and consolidating them into risks, all information captured will be rationalised and details of their source and consequences will be traceable.

10 PROJECT MANAGEMENT IMPROVEMENTS

10.1 PROJECT MANAGEMENT WEAKNESS

In the process of using I.T. Risk Management, it will soon become apparent that probably the main cause for the threatening risks is project management, or perhaps the weakness of individual/s to manage the growth of a system.

Even if you used I.T. Risk Management in its fullest, your experience will soon enable you to identify the real cause for the failure in implementing your system. In such cases, your programme/project management may need further support, assistance, training, better communicational ability and proper delegating, or even some listening to other people involved in the on-going project. Employing the expertise of a consultancy may help.

The main point is to try to reduce potential project caused loss by providing efficient *Event* driven project reviews for the critical project/s. Such project consulting steps will create and utilise virtual group of experienced project managers. As a panel of experts they will assess critical projects and provide consulting being perceived as helpful by the project team, the management, and the users/clients.

10.2 PROCESS STEPS

For such a project consulting programme implementation, various process steps are needed:

1. Select critical project,
2. Understand project status,
3. Plan project review,
4. Create reviews agenda
5. Execute project review,
6. Implement change plan,
7. Conclude the project review.

10.3 INFORMATION COLLECTION

The project manager of the project pending the review should gather the requested information from the existing project documentation. If such documentation is not available, the project manager should collect as much as possible from verbal discussions.

Such a preparation should include details of:

1. Communication plans,

2. Project organisation plan,

3. Contacts and scopes,

4. Background and status of finances,

5. Schedules,

6. Status and history of resources plans,

7. Quality plan,

8. System documentation,

9. Brief description of the project environment,

10. Risk register prioritisation/s and other reports,

11. Last project review minutes.

10.4 RESOURCES AGREEMENT

The final outcome of all communications, discussions and reviews should enable the team members to produce an agreed score on the various project management resources.

The list for such a scoring agreement should include:

1. Quality management,

2. User participation,

3. Requirements management,

4. Communications,

5. Business orientation,

6. Project team,

7. Project planning,

8. Risk management,

9. Technical environment.

10.5 SCORE GRAPH

A scoring card graph can easily be produced on a spreadsheet and it ought to look something like this:

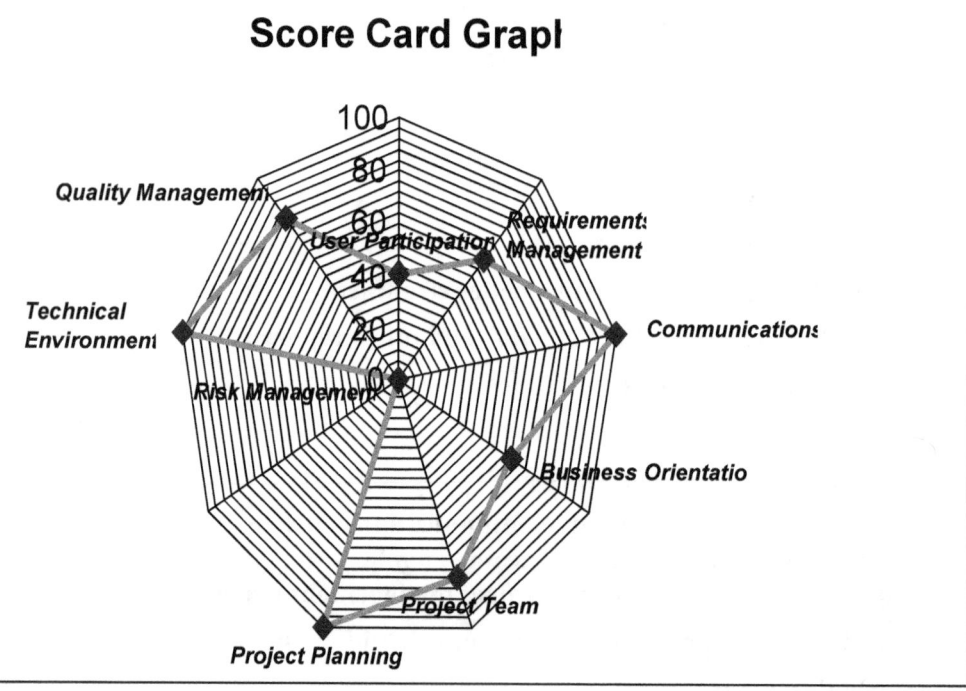

11. I.T. RISKS LOGICAL ANALYSIS POINTS

A risk is an uncertain event which may have an adverse effect on the project's objectives. This Risk Management book is based on a proven risk management methodology, which should be very effective in the quest for identifying risks throughout the project life-cycle.

Remember, this I.T. Risk Management methodology is:

• Forward looking, investigating problems and how to deal with threats,

• A tool enabling communication, getting people at all levels to talk to each other and to interact,

• A no blame team culture, bringing concerns into the open where actions can be taken and plans put in place, in order to stop a risk occurring.

The I.T. Risk Management process commences by identifying the enterprises most important and risky projects, as these must be given priority. This I.T. Risk Management book/manual is essentially a method that permits the collection of knowledge and experience from those involved, in a form that facilitates the Systematic Interaction and Generic Methodology for Applications.

The varied events, their assessments, and the consequential risks relating to or consisting of a system. Methodical in procedures and plans, these are addressed to those involved and deliberating within the parameters of their systems development responsibilities.

The results will depend on interaction. The mutual or reciprocal action which encourages those involved in the programmes and projects to communicate with each other and to work closely with a view to solving the threatening events before they impact on the development of the system. The individuals involved maintain a generic approach, which relates and characterises the whole group of those involved in assessing the events and attacking the threatening ones before they become risks to the development of the system.

The end result being the avoidance of apparent problems within the pre-defined users' systems requirements. This is enabled by following the Risk Management Methodology. The system architects and the risk management practitioners simply follow the approved body of systems development methods, rules and management procedures employed by their organisation. For practical or even ethical reasons, it must be noted that with such a philosophy, it is seldom possible to fulfil all requirements of very large organisational systems.

As such, the risk methodology is administered in applications. Putting to use such techniques and in applying the risk management principles in the development of various applications will involve numerous and varied activities. A concrete issue in developing new applications is the problem of communication among the people involved, the motivation constantly needed for generic work, the ability to interact systematically and in using a structured systems methodology.

END

INDEX OF CONTENTS: PAGE:

SECTION THREE

CHANGES

Andreas Sofroniou

CONTENTS: PAGE:

Change Management and the changes to Configuration, Release, and Assets as a whole group of activities have traditionally been concerned with finding effective solutions to specific operational problems. The purpose of this book is to look at current problems and new, better methods, techniques, and tools for processing changes. In the past, it has been found that too many of the solutions are not implemented and, of those that are, too few survive the inclination of client functional areas to return to familiar ways of doing things. Therefore, Change Management personnel have gradually come to realize that their tasks should not only include solving specific problems but also designing problem-solving and implementation systems that predict and prevent future problems, identify and solve current ones, and implement and maintain these solutions under changing conditions.

As an Executive in multi-national organisations and Government Departments, the author has come to realise that most problems do not arise in isolation but are part of an interacting system. The book, in principle, is seeking for a process of simultaneous interrelated solutions to a set of interdependent problems. Further more, substantial effort has been devoted in recommending a rational methodology for one, or the least possible processes, for future change management. Businesses need to find better ways of doing things, is often not nearly as great as is the need to maximize use of what is already operational. This book, therefore, has been addressing itself more and more to determining how to produce the willingness to change procedures suitable to the way people are willing to work and with processes that they are familiar with.

The book, which follows various consultancy assignments, considers the additional, more detailed recommendations, including strategic changes, training, convincing resources, meetings with people, development of workshops and exchanges of new ideas. The reader, therefore, must consider such points that absorb resources, excessive costs and incur a heavy workload for existing staff.

In the areas in which technology advances fastest, new products and new materials are required in a constant flow, but there are many client areas in which the rate of change can be gentle. Although each process considered may be trivial, the total effect is many times as large as the margin between success and failure in an operational situation. These efforts to improve existing processes have been formalised under the various sections of this book.

The legacy processes and their procedures have had a dramatic impact on the management of changes. The speed and data-handling capabilities of experienced staff, enables the realistic changes and because of their know-how they get meaningful solutions to those changes through the use of long standing techniques. The changes occurring under such circumstances consist of calculating the performance of a system by evaluating a model of it for randomly selected values of variables contained within a unique process and its procedures. Most changes under such operations are concerned with "stochastic" variables; that is, variables whose values change randomly within some probability distribution over time.

There is still considerable difficulty, however, in drawing inferences from operational legacy processes to the real world of smooth Change Management. Additionally, the growing number of changes in the information-processing applications is currently on the increase. To this effect, the recommendations made in this book may be the optimum solution to the problems of adopting new processes. The procedures recommended as processes, will improve the cost-effectiveness of changes and their management. In the realm of the economy, they may be expected to lead to higher productivity, particularly in the service sectors and related processes, decision-making, problem solving, administration, and support of clerical functions.

Awareness that possession of information on any changes is tantamount to a competitive edge is stimulating the gathering of information at national levels. Similarly, concern is mounting over the safeguarding and husbanding of changes to the proprietary and strategic information within the confines of a client, as well as within outsourcing companies. Administration-oriented information systems and the management of changes in client sites have as their objective the husbanding and optimisation of corporate resources, namely; employees and their activities, inventories of materials and equipment, facilities, and finances.

A client's administrative information systems and the Management Information Systems (MIS) focus primarily on resource administration and provide top management with reports of aggregate data. Executive information systems may be viewed as an evolution of administrative information systems in the direction of strategic tracking, modelling, and decision-making. Typically, Change Management consists of a number of processes, each supporting a particular function and changes, which may occur any day of the year.

Change Management processes concentrate on resource allocation and task completion of organized activities. They usually incorporate such scheduling methods as the Critical Path Method (CPM) or Program Evaluation and Review Technique (PERT).

The processes, with which the book is concerned, are first of all man-made. Second, some of them are small and simple to manage, or they are large and complex, depending on the changes required. Their component parts sometimes interact so extensively that a change in one part is likely to affect many others. It is, therefore, of primary importance that all the Change Management processes interact with all the functionalities. Otherwise, Change Management as a tool is of no significance. Processes may also vary depending on the amount of human judgment that enters into their operation.

Programme Management may have many responsibilities, but the most important of all is the ability to identify and positively execute plans to manage the changes threatening the objectives.

Through a process of structured interviews and plans the Assessment Analysis is used to highlight the specific requests for changes, which may turn into risks. During the interviews Assessment Analysis is used to capture the key changes from the interviewees.

In turn, the Assessment Analysis provides a life-cycle process, which highlights the primary prioritisation of the changes. In large, complex, and critical programmes, it is essential that a true prioritised report is available so that the imminent changes can be managed first.

The process commences by identifying the most important changes, which may become threats to a project. These are given priority, support and management expertise. Once the prioritisation exercise is completed, the participating people are notified and subsequently interviewed to bring out and capture any possible changes they may have.

Within a programme, projects are prioritised to ensure that those most critical to the programme's success are given priority to scarce resources.

CHANGE MANAGEMENT METHODOLOGY

The Management of Change allows the capture of collective knowledge and expertise from those involved on the project, in a form that facilitates the communication of changes, their assessments, and the pro-active management of the changes requested.

In essence, this is the mechanism by which the functions of Information Technology programmes and projects are held together as a result of the principles operating within the methodology for the management of change:

• Systematic: The varied Changes, their Assessments and the consequential Risks relating to or consisting of a system. Methodical in procedures and plans, these are addressed to those involved and deliberating within the parameters of their systems development responsibilities.

• Integration: The results being dependable on the mutual or reciprocal action which encourages those involved in the programmes and projects to communicate with each other and to work closely with a view to solving the threatening changes before they impact on the development of the system.

• Generic: The individuals involved maintain an approach, which relates and characterises the whole group of those involved in assessing the changes and attacking any threatening ones before they become risks to the development of the system. The end result being the avoidance of apparent problems within the pre-defined users systems requirements.

• Methodology: Following the system architects and the change management practitioners enable this. Simply follow the approved body of systems development methods, rules and management procedures employed by their organisation. For practical or even ethical reasons, it must be noted that with such a philosophy, it is seldom possible to fulfil all requirements of very large organisational systems.

• Applications: As such, Change Management is administered by putting to use such techniques and in applying the Change Management principles in the development of various applications will involve numerous and varied activities. A concrete issue in developing new applications is the problem of communication among the people involved, the motivation constantly needed for generic work, the ability to interact systematically and in using Change Management.

In general, the Management of Change, deals with the substitution of one thing or set of conditions for another, thus making something different from its previous condition, be it an alteration in state or quality, variety, variation, mutation.

More specific, in the Information Technology environment anything that becomes different, be it the performance of a system, the planning of new enhancements, the development of new systems and their various phases, the complete configuration and its assets, releases, all this require a structure approach.

Change Management in Information Technology Programmes Management, therefore, includes and enables any:

- Alteration,
- Modification,
- Conversion,
- Variance,
- Transformation,
- Remodelling,
- Reconstruction,
- Re-organization,
- Substitution,
- Replacement.

Any kind or type of change which may occur and affect a systems configuration, releases and assets, be it hardware, software or whatever the term of IT may represent.

This process spans the whole life cycle from initial concept and definition of business needs through to the end of the useful life of an asset or end of a services contract. Both conventionally funded and more innovative types of funded projects are included. This definition is consistent with modern supply chain management practices. The process is not limited to the purchasing function in companies and departments and is inherently multi-functional especially in large, complex and/or novel procurements.

CHANGE MANAGEMENT LEADER

The Change Management Leader proposes and agrees the scope of the Change Management processes, function, the items that are to be controlled, and the information that is to be recorded.

Develops Change Management standards, Change Management plans and procedures. Evaluates Change Management tools and recommends those that best meet the organisation's budget, resource, timescale and technical requirements.

Creates and manages the Change Management plan. Performs audits to check that the physical IT inventory is consistent with the Change Management Database Initiates actions needed to secure funds to enhance the infrastructure and staffing levels in order to cope with growth and change

CHANGE MANAGEMENT CYCLE

The concept being a simple one as shown in the diagram below:

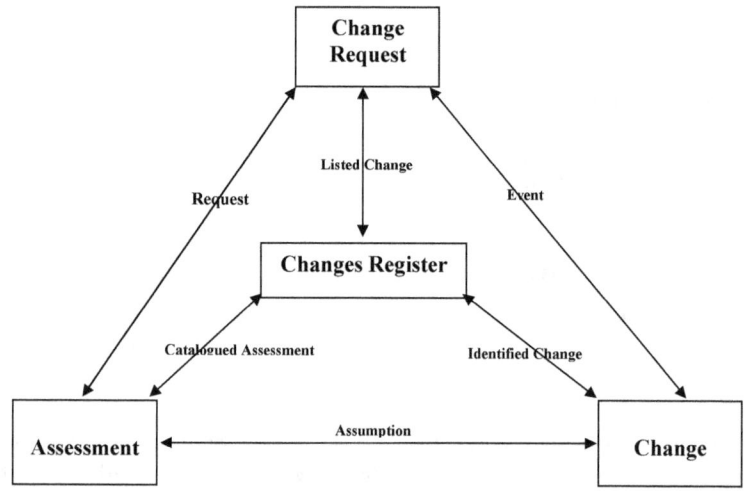

Change Management Cycle

The Change Manag Change Management Cycle in this book were developed by the author whilst employed by *PsySys Limited,* over a period of twenty four years. The methodology was used for PsySys' international clients, from 1980 onwards. The idea of a structured approached to organisational requests for changes and their management proved beneficial to customers and users who integrated the full process with other methodologies, such as Structured Systems Analysis and Designing methods and Project Management procedures.

INTEGRATION OF METHODOLOGIES

The comprehension of how to integrate the three methodologies can be achieved, simply by following the concept as shown below:

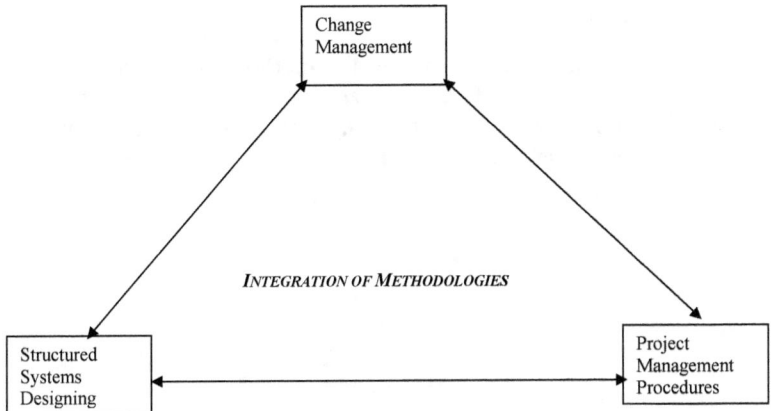

The various steps included in each of the methodologies are named in the next diagram. Or, to a further extent, the various stages of system development and the steps taken to manage projects and adopt the change management cycle, are shown on the next page:

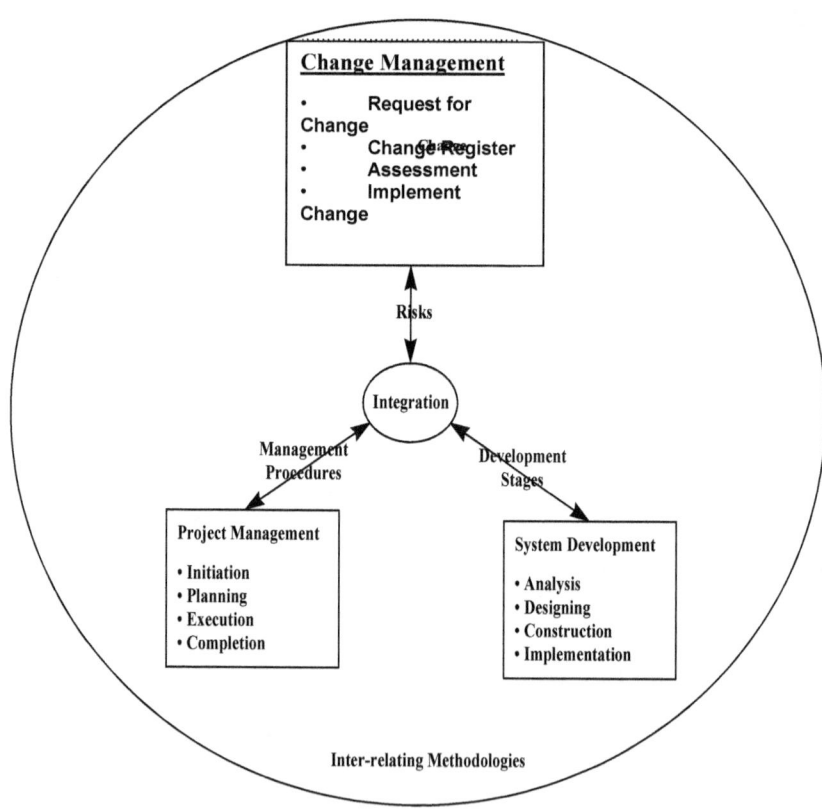

It is basic business sense to identify, assess, manage, and monitor changes that are significant to the fulfilment of an organisation's business objectives. In recent years businesses have been transformed by, and are in many cases heavily dependent on I.T.

The financial consequences of a breakdown in controls or a security breach are not only the loss incurred, but also the costs of recovering and preventing further failures. The impact is not only financial: it can affect adversely reputation and brand value as well as the business' performance and future potential.

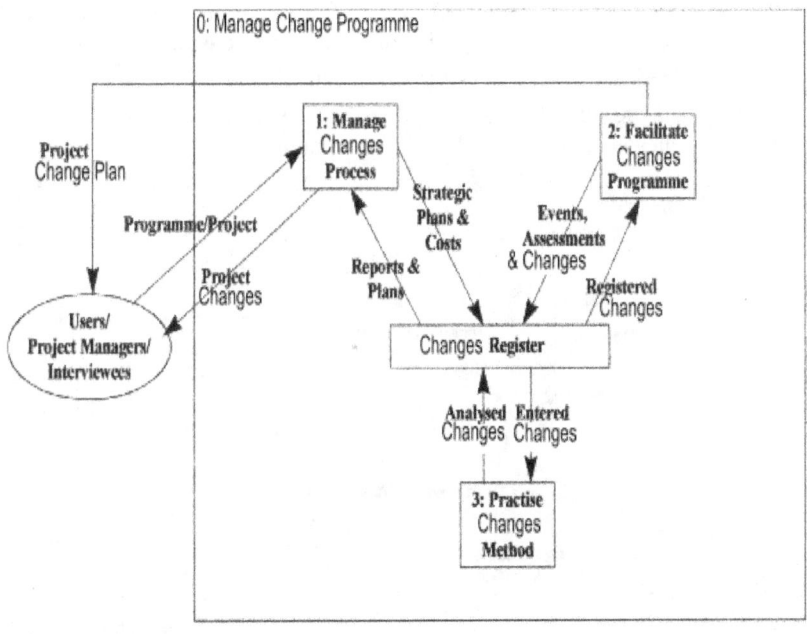

Boards can regard inadequate system development as a significant risk, and where directors feel that this may be the situation in their organisations, they may need to ask tough questions of themselves and their management teams. Systems development and their changes is an issue that boards may need to recognise should regularly be on their agenda, and not delegated to I.T. technicians.

Business in the past was primarily confined to assessment of the change and its associated risk surrounding fire, flood, and Acts of God. In business today we have become high dependent on information systems. Failure to build computer systems as required and the changes requested thereafter, by the users has a major impact on our business to function. The inability of companies to provide adequate systems can cause potential problems to customers, suppliers, employees and an all round havoc to information.

To build a complete picture of what the Change Management cycle includes, please refer to the diagram drawn below:

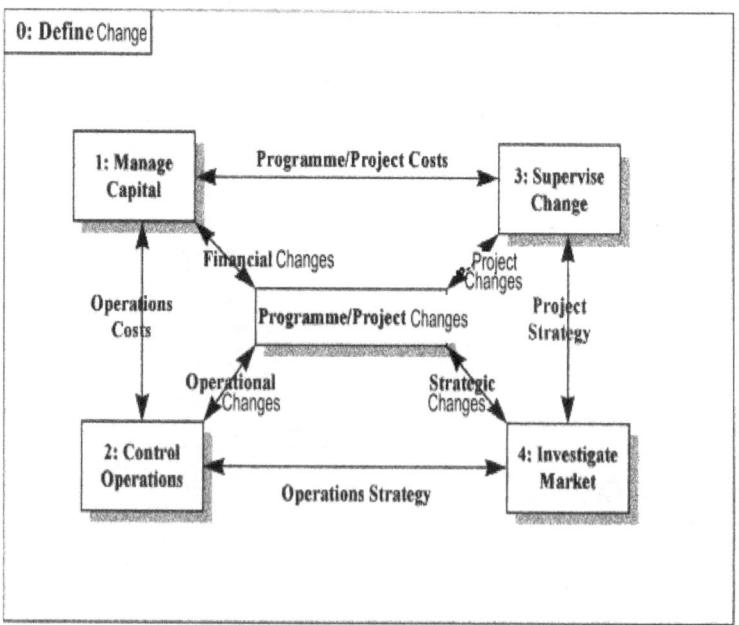

The Components Of The Total Business Changes

Fundamental to the creation of a Change Management system is the assessment of the changes (Changes Analysis) to your business and the potential loss that could accrue if things go wrong. Change Assessment software tools are available in the market, which can be used by consultants, or by internal staff. What is important is the ability to assess the change to your business and the cost to protect it against the change. The end result is that you have to make the valued judgement on the amount the business spends, on the implementation and the monitoring of a change policy.

Products and systems are available to counter the threats and changes that have been identified. There is a wide range of options available, but remember that anything chosen will require expertise to design and complete a system, taking into account how the various solutions will inter-react with each other. Like all things to do with I.T., the design and implementation of systems, change solutions are only as good as the people installing them.

COMMUNICATION

The most important factor in the success of any management style is the ability to communicate with each other, one to one or in groups of people. The art of communication is just as important to the whole process of the management of changes. More so, where the changes identified have become a threat because of the problem of human communications.

This is where the appointment of an experienced and trained Change Practitioner is worth the effort put into securing such individual/s.

CHANGE MANAGEMENT PRACTICE

A trained Change Management Practitioner will have enough knowledge to run and maintain the system, as well as ample experience to be able to communicate with all levels of employees, hold meetings, and ensure the plans executed.

In brief and as the diagram on the next page shows, the Practitioner will be responsible for the complete Change Management cycle.

In analysing changes, certain counter measures may have to be looked into. The mechanisms for safeguarding the construction of your information system are by managing changes and avoiding the threat of failing to build the required system.

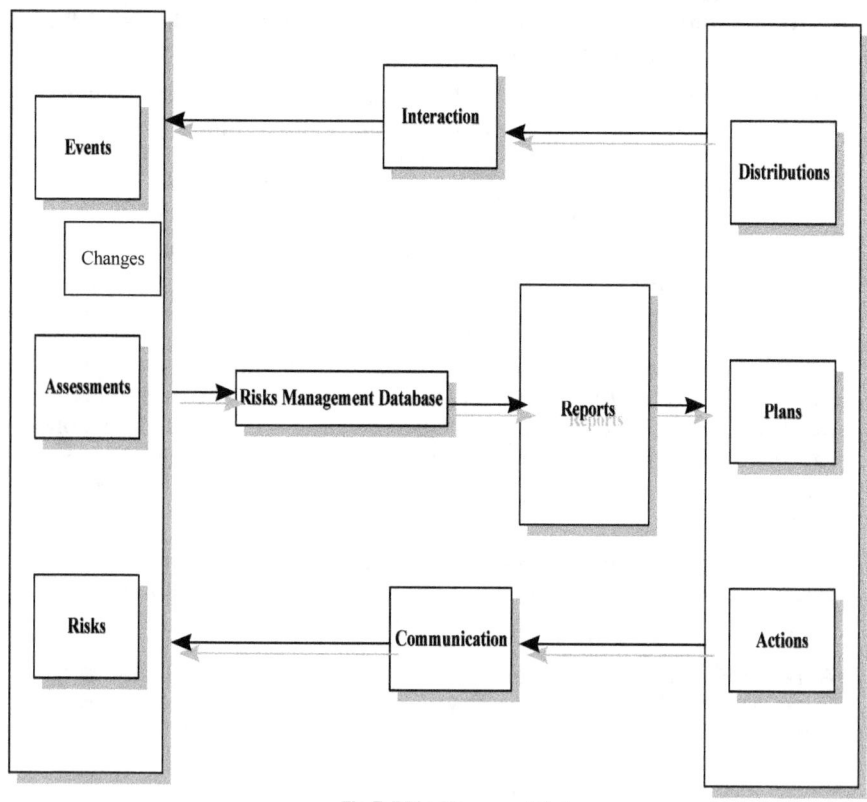

The Full Risk Management Cycle

Programme Objectives

It is a fact that most large, complex projects and programs fail to meet their planned objectives and as a consequence, most organisations are undertaking one or more aggressive programs at any point in time. These may fundamentally change the way the company conducts its business and failure to meet objectives on time may lead to a catastrophic loss of business.

Some projects or programmes can be chaotic at times. Objectives are evolving and plans and priorities are constantly changing. There is a temptation to accept this chaos as a necessary 'nature of the beast'. However, it is essential to move the programme forward in a traditional project management way by making sure that objectives and plans move forward.

Once we have clear objectives and plans, programme managers must control two fundamental factors if they are to be successful:

- The business plan must be clearly identified,
- The implementation of the program must be made explicit.

This can be answered by isolating the fundamental cause of most, if not all-major project problems. It can be argued that projects only fail due to two fundamental reasons:

- The plans are proven to be incorrect,
- The significance of these plans is misunderstood.

The capture, analysis, and communication of such assessments are, therefore, critical to the success of any project. This forms the basis of the Change Management method. This method has been applied by PsySys Limited to help many diverse organisations to deliver large, complex projects and programmes on time, to budget and in meeting the expectations of demanding users.

Suggested Method

The focus of the method is based on he capture and analysis of the critical events and their assessments within the project plans, processes, and procedures.

The method is essentially a framework process that allows the capture of collective knowledge and viewpoints from those involved on the project, in a form that facilitates communication of events, assessments and ensures the pro-active management of changes. This is accomplished by dramatically improving communications, risks (which may be caused by changes) are avoided or managed to the optimum, and project objectives are delivered on time.

In essence, this is the mechanism by which the functions of programmes and projects are held together as a result of the principles operating within the method.

This, in effect, includes the varied events, their assessments and the consequential changes relating to or consisting of a system. Methodical in procedures and plans, these are addressed to those involved and deliberating within the parameters of their systems development responsibilities.

The results being dependable on the mutual or reciprocal action which encourages those involved in the programmes and projects to communicate with each other and to work closely with a view to solving the threatening events before they impact on the development of the system.

The individuals involved maintain an approach, which relates and characterises the whole group of those involved in assessing the events and attacking the threatening ones before any changes become risks to the development of the system.

Following the system architects and the change management practitioners enables this. Simply follow the approved body of systems development methods, rules and management procedures employed by their organisation. For practical or even ethical reasons, it must be noted that with such a philosophy, it is seldom possible to fulfil all requirements of very large organisational systems.

As such, the suggested method is administered in the various applications. Putting to use such techniques and in applying the change management principles in the development of various applications will involve numerous and varied activities. A concrete issue in developing new applications is the problem of communication among the people involved, the motivation constantly needed for generic work, the ability to interact systematically and in using a structured systems methodology.

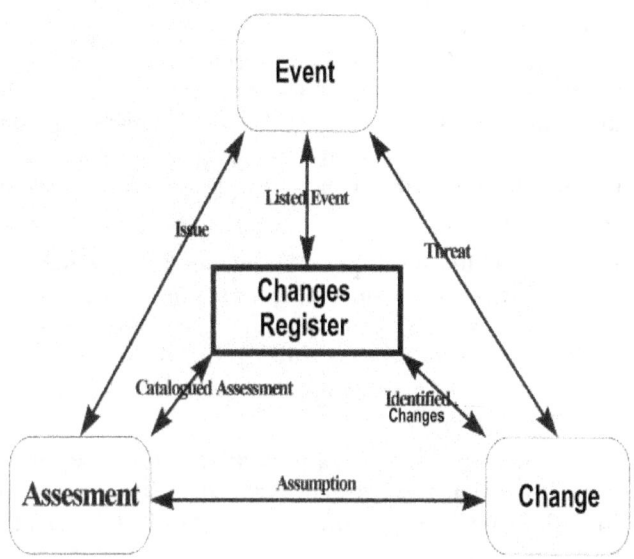

Change Management Cycle

FEATURES OF THE APPROACH

The key features and benefits of the PsySys Limited approach are:

• *Communication* — Provides a simple, common, language for the communication of risk up, down and sideways within the organisation, whilst avoiding the normal problems of political sensitivity and risk aversion.

• *Control* — Enhances project control by exception management and achieves an overview of change at senior management levels.

• *Information* — Encourages the sharing of change information, establishing common objectives, discouraging change transfer and hence reducing the overall risk to all involved parties.

• *Flexible* — An adaptable process, which is rigorously applied to ensure that all significant changes are identified and controlled at the appropriate time.

• *Acceptable* — The non-intrusive/non-bureaucratic management process improves management discipline across the organization and is readily accepted by project teams.

ASSESSMENT ANALYSIS

The core of *Change* is in the Assessment Analysis. This uses structured techniques to analyse project plans and identify the most sensitive events that are potentially unstable, and therefore the source of greatest change.

Everything is rated on a GAR principle: <u>G</u>reen, <u>A</u>mber and <u>R</u>ed scale; where G is always "good" and R is always "bad". This provides an instantly understood assessment on each stage: Events, Assessments, and Changes in relationship with the time scales as used in the plans. This, effectively, provides guidance on how best to handle the change.

STRATEGIC COST ANALYSIS

Costing is a process within the approach that can be used to define the cost of a requested change within a project or business area from as early as the proposal stage. It works by adding a 'quality' dimension to the estimating process so that high quality estimates, based on relevant experience, are treated differently from low quality estimates, which are little more than guesses.

The output takes the form of a probability distribution diagram and a set of assessments, which need to be managed in order to move the curve to the left and squeeze it (i.e. reduce the likely cost and the uncertainty).

Costing is particularly useful in the early stages of a project when the final cost of the project is subject to great uncertainty. The process has also been effectively used to define business budgets for re-structured business areas.

ADMINISTRATION SYSTEM TOOL

A Microsoft Access based tool or any type of an ordinary spreadsheet can be utilised to allow the events, assessments and changes to be captured and reviewed by all stockholders in the program. In this way changes that would have been missed are captured through the identification of events.

WORK PLAN ANALYSIS

Work Plan Analysis is a set of techniques that enables a rapid change assessment to be undertaken on a complex project, which is already in progress.

It is always difficult to focus on the right areas when the project organisation is large and the plans are extensive and likely to be multi-levelled. Using Work Plan Analysis, the 'poor quality' areas of a project are quickly highlighted for further investigation.

One very successful application of this approach has been through the use of Project Readiness Assessment Walkthroughs. These are structured review meetings held just prior to major project milestones or deliverables. Initially the project team explain their self-evaluation of the project status and are questioned by an independent review team. Potential changes arising are captured using the Assessment Analysis process.

COMMUNICATING CHANGES

The technique summarised above will only deliver its full benefits to any business if a suitable governance structure is quickly established to communicate the change information and set suitable actions to mitigate the changes. The mapping of the process onto an organisation is the key step to ensuring that the investment in the process is fully realised.

TEAM APPROACH

An enterprise must escape from a culture based on transfer of changes between parties, to a team approach that is focused on implementing changes. Methods must be effective without the need for detailed time-consuming analysis.

DEFINITION OF A CHANGE

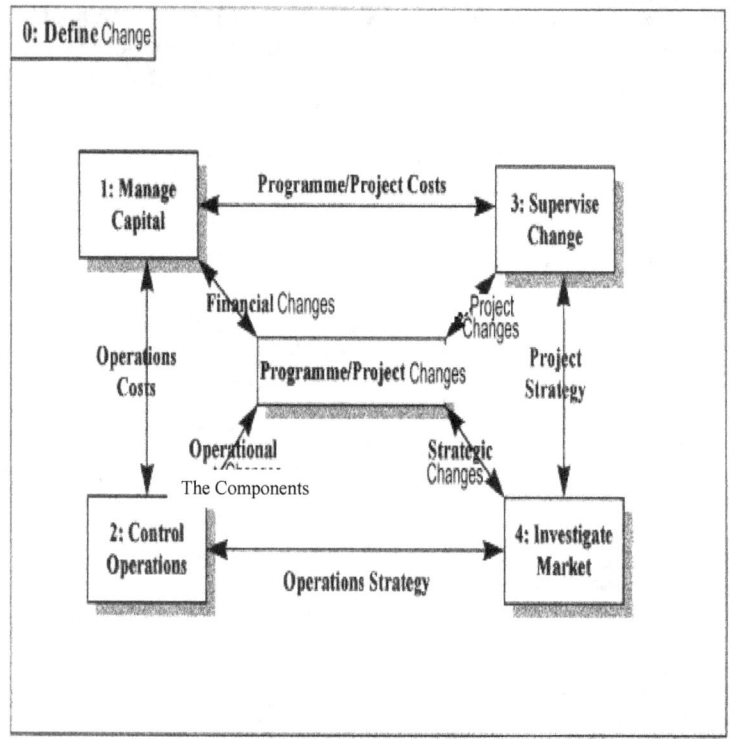

The Comp[onents Of The Total Business Changes

A change may be perceived as a possible loss. A change is individual to a person or organisation because another as a minor change may perceive what one individual as a major change perceives.

A change is linked very strongly with competitiveness. Each decision has the possibility of resulting in loss. Each decision to introduce a new product into the marketplace can result in varying degrees of loss or gain. To be entrepreneurial is to accept change, that is, the possibility of loss. A good entrepreneur's strength, however, is to make decisions which maximise possible gain. Hence minimise possible loss, which constitutes effective change management.

Change is inherent in all aspect of an organisation and may be viewed from four primary directions: financial, operational, programme/project and portfolio/products. Many changes are related to the running of the operations and its processes but are often in trying to change operations that the greatest change is experienced. It is the management of change in such 'change' projects that the method (explained earlier) addresses.

A project can be described in its simplest terms as: Planning to achieve specific objectives and then executing the plans. The emphasis is on the word 'plan' as without a plan we have no project. So in the context of a project, a change is something, which might disrupt the plans such that the objectives of the project are not met. The discipline of Project Change Management is thus a framework of techniques, which allows the project manager to pro-actively identify and manage changes before they develop into problems, which will impact the project plans.

APPROACHES TO CHANGE MANAGEMENT

In recent years we have seen large projects in many areas of business suffering from a lack of control. The size of cost and time over-runs do not seem to be decreasing, despite the amount of management time which is being dedicated to analysing and quantifying the potential problems and selecting suitable personnel and processes. One may conclude that management, either do not have the correct methods and tools in place to attack the potential problems, or that they are not using, or do not understand, those which they do have.

In the early 1970's, the concepts of formal project change management began to emerge. Hailed as the saviour of project managers, in practice the results have been mixed. Change management has proved highly effective in certain mature industries - e.g. the Petrochemical or construction industry where project managers can base their estimates on years of similar engineering experience. Difficulties seem to be encountered when these traditional Change Management methods are applied to innovative and fast evolving areas such as Information Technology.

EVENTS AND CHANGE REGISTER

Most projects will have an Events Register and some may have what they call a Change Register. In effect, this tends to be a list into which anyone can input the concerns. It will contain references to current problems, questions, and assessments, difficult activities about which there is reasonable confidence and the odd real change.

In any large project the Events or Change Register quickly becomes swamped with items that require very different actions and many which do not require any action at all. All this leads to an inevitable loss of focus. Further, the content tends to be biased towards current problems rather than future potential problems.

INDIVIDUAL INTERVIEWS

One-on-one interviews can be an effective way of capturing changes. When management and peers do not inhibit people, they tend to be far more open about their concerns. Unfortunately, most use very unsophisticated approaches such as "what do you see as your changes?" or "what keeps you awake at night?" Thus, if the person being interviewed is sensitive to discussing changes it may prevent the capture of any valuable information. At best the changes captured will tend to lack structure, as they are not focused onto the future objectives that the project plans to achieve.

GROUP BRAINSTORMING

Can be a very effective technique for opening up a very complex situation. However, information can be subconsciously suppressed by peer pressure, which may bias the discussion on one area at the expense of the rest of the project. Inevitably the mass of information captured is often difficult to focus, prioritise and allocate ownership.

In general, it should be remembered that the quality of the output is only as good as the quality of the input data.

CHANGE ANALYSES AND QUANTIFICATION

Changes may be difficult to capture reliably and concisely but further problems are likely to be experienced when trying to analyse them. Virtually all approaches to change analysis are based on estimating the factored impact of the change. This exposure to change is a combination of the chance (probability) of an event happening and the consequences (impact) if it does occur i.e.:

- Change Exposure = Potential Impact x Probability of Occurrence

Fundamental problems arise when individuals are required to estimate, numerically, the impact and then predict (numerically) the probability. Estimates, which are often little more than guesses, result in a single point estimate of Change Exposure, which is then given undeserved credibility in the detailed analysis of the change and used as the basis for many major project decisions. Also, it is often the case that part of the change impact can be quantified but often not the major part. An example can be based on an attempt to quantify bad publicity, quality, and relationship.

Some processes add complexity by rating the impact of changes in terms of financial, time scales, quality, performance etc., which quickly become very tedious to maintain.

CHANGE CONTROL AND LACK OF FOLLOW-THROUGH

Many change management systems fail due to a lack of follow-through on actions. There is a surprising tendency to identify changes and then watch them happen!

This is caused by:

- Failure to use the change register to set appropriate action plans,

- Lack of regular updates/maintenance of the change register,

- Absence of named owners and deadlines (lack of ownership),

- Tracking generalities rather than specifics,

- Concentrating on what can be done if the change occurs rather than stopping the change happening (pro-active),

- Trying to transfer the change elsewhere, without considering the consequences.

CHANGE TRANSFER

Change transfer often occurs because the partner who knows most about the level of change within the enterprise (i.e. the supplier/purchaser relationship) is encouraged to transfer this to the other partner. Once accomplished, the party with the most knowledge of the change relaxes and the most ignorant partner inherits the change. An example of this is the Purchaser insisting on a fixed-price contract in a poorly defined contract when they know that the supplier does not understand the scope of the contract.

The supplier then has a tendency to deliver the minimum possible and obtain sign-off for everything, irrespective of quality. The effect of this type of commercial 'table-tennis' is actually to increase the level of change within the enterprise as the real changes pile up without intervention.

What is needed is a method that identifies and encourages the attack of real change at source. Such a method would force projects within the enterprise to become pro-active by attacking risky changes, rather than waiting for events to unfold and then counting the cost, as recorded in the previous month's financial returns.

CHANGE MANAGEMENT VS. PROJECT MANAGEMENT

There is often a tendency to treat change management as no more than another necessary evil of project management. Thus, it often becomes an additional administrative burden for the Project Manager and consequently does not get the quality attention to make it work effectively.

In order to make change management work, a shift in philosophy is required. This must lead the project team to view the process not just as another component of project management, but more as the communication stabiliser that holds the project together.

PROCESS METHOD

The Change Management method described in this book aims to provide an effective means of managing changes within all types of projects. The process grew out of a thorough assessment of the problems often encountered in project management and the techniques of the traditional change management approaches that have been used to try and improve the situation.

Both good and bad principles were noted and new techniques were introduced to address key deficiencies. The resulting change management process has a proven track record of delivering tangible results in large projects across a diverse range of organisations.

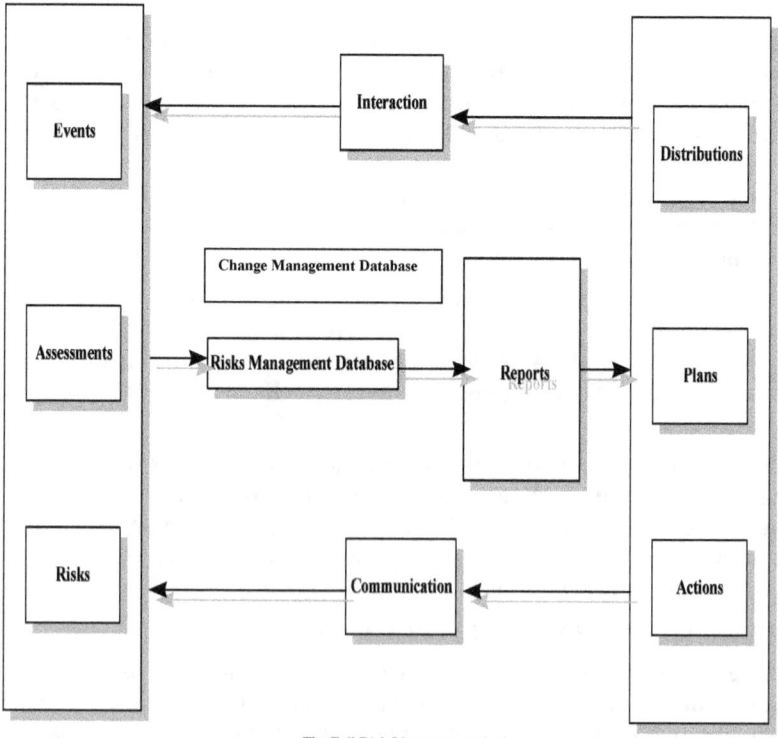

The Full Risk Management Cycle

The stage and status of the project will have a strong bearing on the change management initiation process. Although all situations are unique, the following may give some helpful guidelines. Such a status may make a Strategic Cost Analysis very attractive. If there are no plans it may be difficult to undertake a full Assessment Analysis, but a high level assessment of issues or assumptions based on major milestones should be possible. Expect to identify a high proportion of changes that relate to missing or inadequate plans and resources problems. Projects just starting tend to have many events and few assessments (due to the lack of documented plans).

PLANNED PROJECT

Once the project has been substantially planned and is active, Assessment Analysis becomes the primary change identification process. If the planning is very detailed and/or complex, some of the techniques of Work Plan Analysis may prove useful. For example, if there were a requirement to produce a first-cut of a change register very quickly, for a rapidly approaching milestone, a Project Readiness Walkthrough would be an ideal approach.

TROUBLED PROJECT

The key aspect of a project in trouble is that it requires re-planning to put it back on track. Thus, the timing of the change assessment relative to this planning process is very important.

If the re-planning process has not started there will be very little of the new approach to assess. It may be possible to influence this new approach by undertaking a change assessment of the options being considered. To do this an Assumption Analysis of the alternative high-level plans can provide a useful framework for decision-making.

If the project has been re-planned, then an Assessment Analysis of the new plans, possibly supplemented by Work Plan Analysis, is an appropriate way forward.

INTERVIEWING KEY PEOPLE

Identifying the right people to interview is critical to producing a comprehensive and coherent picture of the changes facing a project. So, to decide on who should be interviewed, start with the project or programme organisational structure.

Depending on the scope of the change assessment (i.e. single project, programme of multiple projects, portfolio of business projects etc.) it may be necessary to map the organisational hierarchy to ensure that the right people are interviewed and that the changes arising are reviewed at an appropriate level.

Working with the Programme or Project Manager, try to identify the 'key players'. A key player is someone within the programme/project who is likely to have either specific expertise in a particular area and/or insight into the environment in which the project is being implemented.

Key players tend to be Project Managers for a programme or Team Managers for a project with the addition of Users involved in the requirement capture and other activities. This group would likely form the initial interview list.

During the interview, these people should decide who else is needed to participate. Interviewers need to exercise their judgement when evaluating the responses to this question. Typically it is necessary to go down at least one level below the Project/Team manager unless the team size is small.

One of the key features of this process is that of obtaining counter viewpoints within the organisation. Thus, the more people interviewed the better. However, if many projects are being assessed for change within an organisation, resource constraints will inevitably lead to reducing the interview pool. Under these circumstances at least two counter viewpoints must be obtained within each project. (Business manager and technical manager) so that the assessment ratings can be compared.

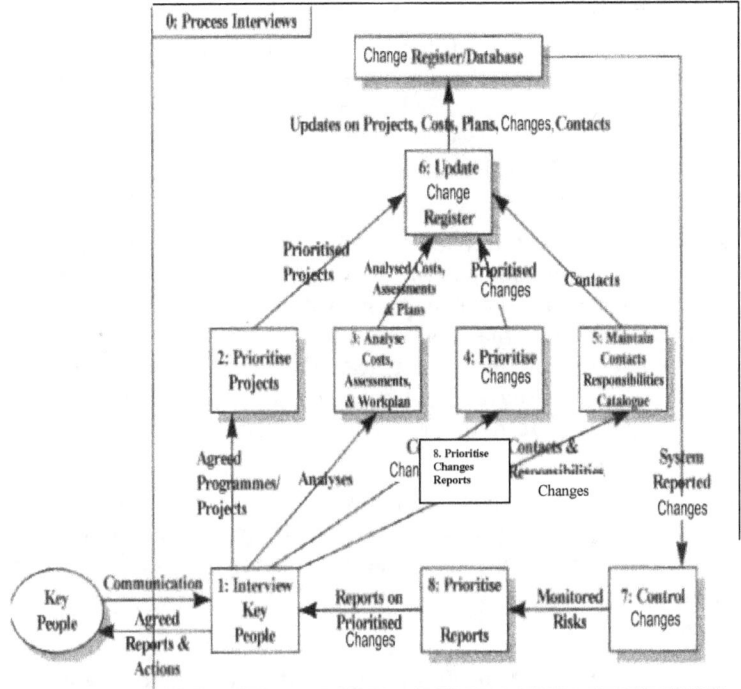

THE INTERVIEWING PROCESS

SUITABLE CHANGE ASSESSMENT TEAM

• The team that will operate and manage the process requires a particular set of skills and background to be successful:

• Experience of working in large (preferably non-consulting) projects and managing (preferably) medium sized projects (say 10-20 people).

• Understanding of project planning principles and some exposure to associated tools.

• Forceful personalities to ensure quality data captures in difficult client situations.

• IT background, in order to understand the issues in IT projects and to help with using the support tools.

• Some understanding of the clients business.

Note that it can sometimes be a disadvantage to have too much knowledge of the clients business in applying the process. This is because there may be a tendency ₜₒr the interviewer to get into too much detail in non-risky areas and take too much of the client's time in the process.

After the initial round of interviews, a suitable forum must be established to discuss the changes identified. The client may suggest that the changes are discussed as part of the regular project meeting. This should be resisted unless the changes are an early agenda item and there will be sufficient time to get through the agenda with this additional discussion.

Typically, a minimum of an hour will be required for discussion of the changes - all if possible but just the most critical if not. If discussion of the changes is left to the end there will often be little time (or concentration) left to do the process justice. Also, it is likely that some events will end up being discussed twice. If discussed first, the changes tend to focus the meeting and get away from talking about progress onto the things that need to be discussed - i.e. what threatens the success of the project.

The best method is to establish a specific Change Review Meeting with a representation consisting of the Change Owners and chaired by the Programme Director, or the process 'champion' in the client organisation.

CHANGE PRIORITISATION

Prioritisation allows the Project Manager to direct limited resources at the most critical project changes.

The objective of the change prioritisation is to identify the most significant changes out of all those, which have been identified by the various analysis methods used. Once all the changes have been collected in a consolidated list or register, they should be placed in order of priority and attacked via a logical, planned programme. The problem is to decide how to place changes in an appropriate order.

ASSESSMENTS AND CHANGES REGISTER

All assessments captured should be held in an Assessments Register. Only critical assessments will be converted into changes and held in a Change Register. Filtering the assessments and consolidating them into changes do this. All information captured will be rationalised and details of their source and consequences will be traceable.

POSITIONING CHANGES

The primary criteria used for prioritising changes are:

- Criticality
- Timing
- Controllability

CRITICALITY

In certain instances the change may undermine the basic objectives of the project and no amount of money will save the project if such a change impacts. If not resolved, the uncertainty may halt the progress of the project. Such a change may be related to the overall programme, a part of the programme, an individual part of the design, or even a particular module of software. This, also, provides a way of representing the effect of such changes on the overall project, where cost impact is small or meaningless.

To satisfy this need a Criticality index is defined. Criticality is in effect a multi-dimensional change impact rating. Once again, we use the assessment A, B, C. C being dangerous, while A impacts the edge of the system design or the programme. Something that may be important in itself, or to one group of users, or designers, but will not stop progress on the rest of the project.

In most applications, Criticality has been the primary means of prioritising changes and has been described in terms of traffic-light ratings of Red, Amber, or Green. This can be very effective at concentrating on the project impacts and/or avoiding confusion with ratings of assessment Sensitivity.

TIMING

One of the most important things we need to know is *when* we have to do something about an event, assessment, or change. In the case of a project we need to know when the change will start to impact the work. Then we must determine when we have to take action to prevent it happening or to reduce its impact. The timing of a change should always equate to the latest time to start the first necessary action. In this respect, it is analogous with trying to stop a cancer. This must be done at the point that it starts to grow.

CONTROLLABILITY

Controllability is a measure of confidence that the change will be managed. It should not be confused with the probability of the change occurring, which is a measure of how likely the change is to occur if nothing is done. The controllability grade cannot normally be assigned until the change has been reviewed and discussed by senior management, whereby an agreement is reached as to their confidence that the change can ultimately be managed. A 'C' grade means that no change plans are in place and no action has been taken, whereas an 'A' grade indicates that change plans or actions are well under way with a very high confidence of success.

Impact Diagrams provide an overview or change profile of the project. However, the detail of the changes is required for the change review meeting in order that the detail of the changes can be seen, discussed and actions taken.

The order of the changes in the report is important so that senior management can focus on the key changes first.

If the impact diagram is used to prioritise the change register the time element can be easily included. For instance there may be an urgent AMBER criticality, C controllability change that needs attention that is not an obvious priority if the Change Report is prioritised by Criticality and Controllability alone.

In essence the easiest way to prioritise is to use the Impact Diagram and to treat the highest priority change as the one nearest to the origin, the next nearest being number two and so on. The intention is to order the risks so that they are roughly in the right order.

CHANGE CONTROL

Changes may be attacked at both the strategic and tactical levels. Strategic approaches look for trends and underlying causes for groups of changes. Tactical approaches take each change at face value.

STRATEGIC APPROACHES

A strategic viewpoint is achieved by using the Change Driver approach. Each assessment and subsequent change is categorised into Technical, Milestone, Decision or Resource to reflect what is driving the poor quality ratings:

• Technical relates to assessments of a technical or complexity nature (e.g. the pure complexity of providing an interface)

• Milestone that applies to assessments regarding timescale dependencies on other projects, or external suppliers, and can be used to identify linkages to project milestones (e.g. an activity which is not inherently complex but may not be feasible due to timescale constraints).

• Decision that is used to describe assessments that require business decisions, business policies or standards (e.g. organisational announcements).

• Resources that relate to resource deficiencies or priorities (e.g. insufficient training resources).

Note that with this categorisation, Policy has been split into Decision and Resource categories. This is necessary when the resource constraints are external to the programme/organisation. When the resource constraints are internal, a simple Policy Driver will cover this.

Categorising assessments and changes in this way identifies the main change drivers, can simplify the identification of trends and assist in the development of appropriate change plans.

For example, Red Decision and Resource changes are "show-stoppers" which generally require senior management action. Red Milestone changes are an indication of how tightly the programme is being "squeezed" and Red Technical changes indicate the complexity of the planned activities.

The Change Driver chart indicates where particular effort is required. In the example below the relatively high number of Decision based changes suggests that the project is being put at risk by having to wait for decisions, probably from within the organisation. A steering committee meeting could potentially resolve most of these changes. If the project is in the early stages, it is already showing signs that the time scales are too ambitious by the high number of milestone changes.

	Technical	Milestone	Resource	Decision	Total
Red	7	15	4	19	45
Amber	12	19	15	26	72
Green	10	6	12	12	40
Total	29	40	31	57	157

It is important to note that noting that the "normal" Change Driver profile trends with the phase of the project. i.e. "Normal" would be (using relative terms):

Phase	Technical	Milestone	Resource	Decision
Start of project	Rising	Min.	Max.	Max.
Middle of project	Max.	Rising	Falling	Falling
End of project	Falling	Max.	Min.	Min.

TACTICAL APPROACHES

Most changes will need to be addressed specifically (i.e. one action plan for each change) to address the underlying assessment. Assessments that are placed in the C area of the Sensitivity/Stability matrix are unreliable, represent significant risks, and it is dangerous to continue with the project without taking action. We must do at least one of two things:

• Stabilise them by escalating the assessment to senior management and obtaining agreements that increase confidence that the assessment will turn out to be true.

• Make the project less sensitive to the assessment i.e. Reduce sensitivity by redesign, re-planning or having acceptable fallback plans in place.

The actions taken to attack the problem may be very different, depending on whether we are trying to reduce Sensitivity or Stabilise. It is normal to try to stabilise the assessment first before trying to handle sensitivity, which is usually more difficult.

FOLLOWING THROUGH ON ACTIONS

Just as it is possible to introduce change by planning a project badly, it is possible to address many changes by using normal project management methods, as long as the risk has been identified early enough.

Changes generally come from two areas activities that have not been planned adequately or planned activities that are likely to go wrong. Therefore, the first filter to apply to the changes is to identify those that can be tackled by just improving the plans. Obviously, if there is no project plan the change is unbounded and the first action must be to create a plan.

NEED FOR CHANGE PLANS

Changes, which cannot be resolved by improved planning, must be tackled individually through the use of dedicated Change Plans. Ultimately, the plans for reducing the changes must be incorporated into the main project plans.

Change Plans may be divided into "Simple" or "Complex", irrespective of the potential impact of the change. Simple means that it is possible to resolve the change quickly say by a simple phone call or single task. For such changes, monitoring the status on the Change Report is sufficient and minimises bureaucracy. Complex changes require significant resources and time to resolve them and for these a formal Change Plan is required.

The diagrammatic flow shown below is the desired overall integration of related top-level processes:

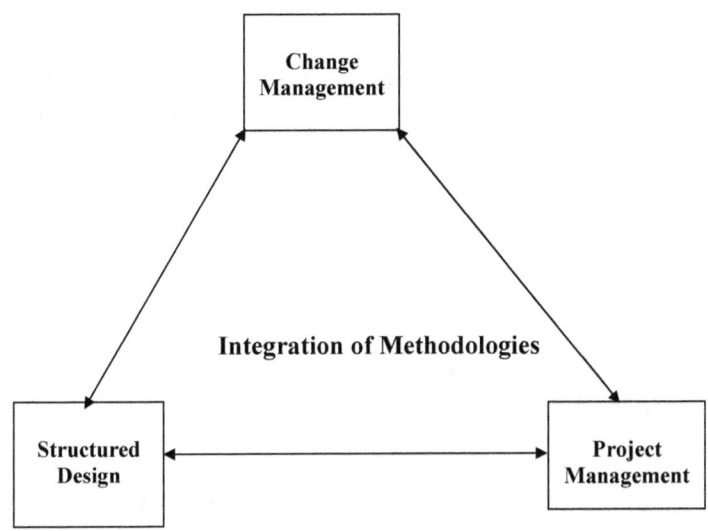

The suggested interfacing of the Structured Systems Analysis and Design methodology and the Project Management procedures to the Change Management processes may be done separately.

In interfacing the various processes from the different existing organisational methodologies, the main steps of Project Management and the Structures Systems Analysis and Designing methodology, will be incorporated in this exercise.

Namely, the four main stages of system development:

- **Analyse,**
- **Design,**
- **Construct,**
- **Implement.**

The identified processes of Project Management procedures and Structured Systems Analysis and Designing to be linked to the Change Management processes of:

- Events,
- Assessments,
- Changes,
- Plans.

The actual points of interfacing the stages of development, the procedures of managing projects and the assessments analysis of the methodology are explored in this book.

PROJECT TO CHANGE MANAGEMENT

Regarding the connections of the project management procedures to change management, it is suggested that the link be from the higher level of project management work elements, such as:

- Initiate Change Management,
- Adjust Project Approach to Change,
- Control Change,
- Complete Change Management.

This is as far as most users drill into the process and generally as far as they are required to by structured analysis and designing methodologies guidelines.

DIAGRAMMATIC REPRESENTATION SHOWN

- **O: Change Management Decomposition,**
- **O: Management of the Change Programme,**
- **1: Managing of the Change Management Process,**
- **2: Facilitation of the Change Management Programme,**
- **3. Practising the Methodology.**

O: Change Management Decomposition

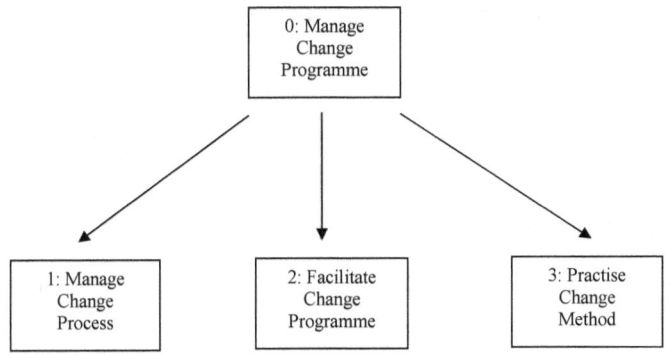

The Change Management Decomposition

The next four Dataflow Diagrams are shown on the following two pages and are:

0: Manage Change Programme,

1: Manage Change Process,

2: Facilitate Change Programme,

3: Practise Change Methodology.

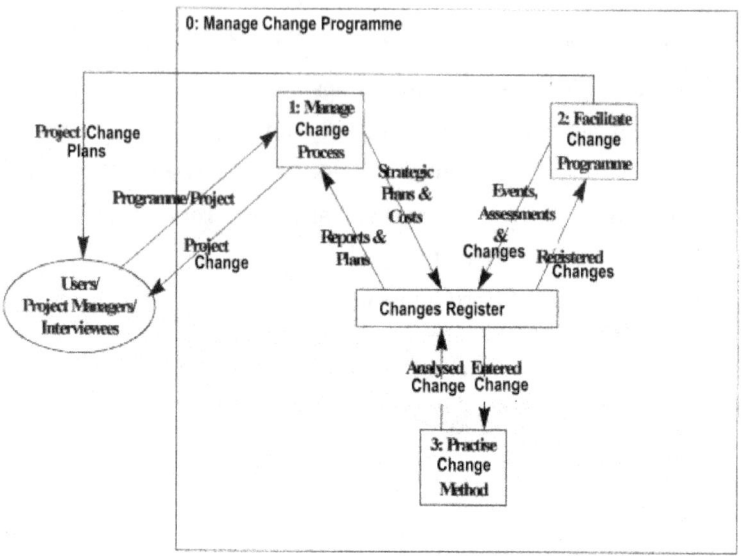

13.4 1: Managing of the Change Management Process

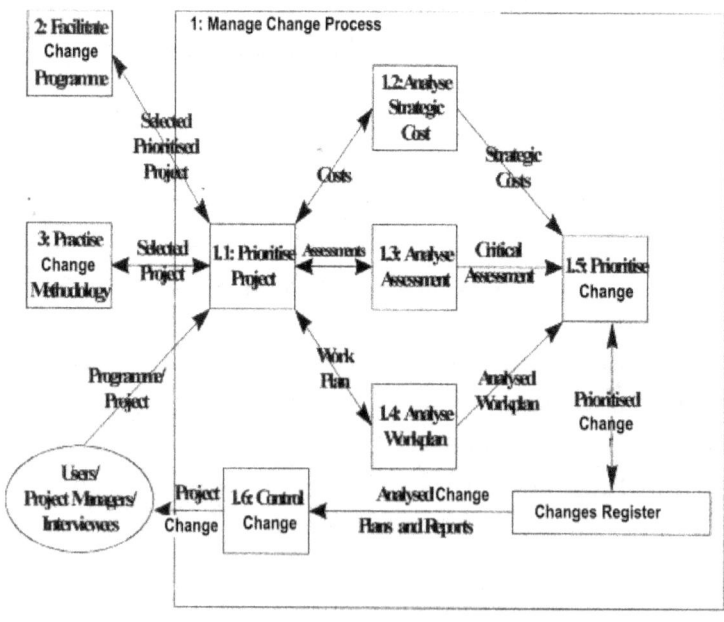

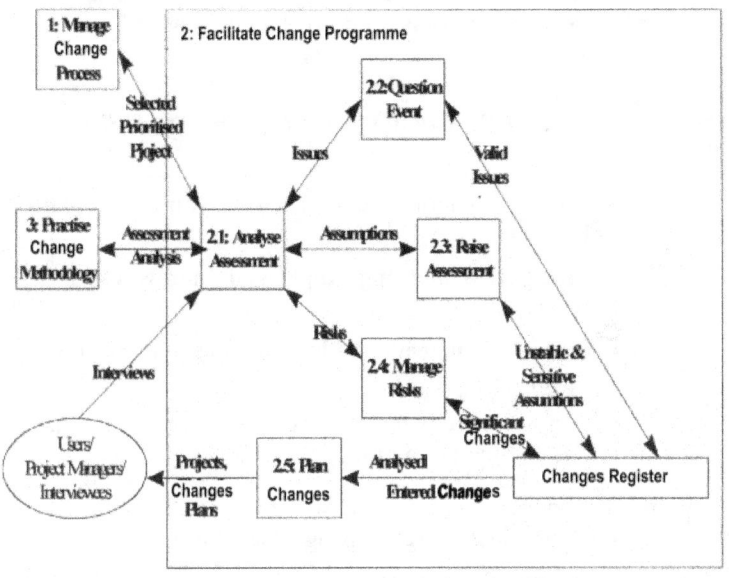

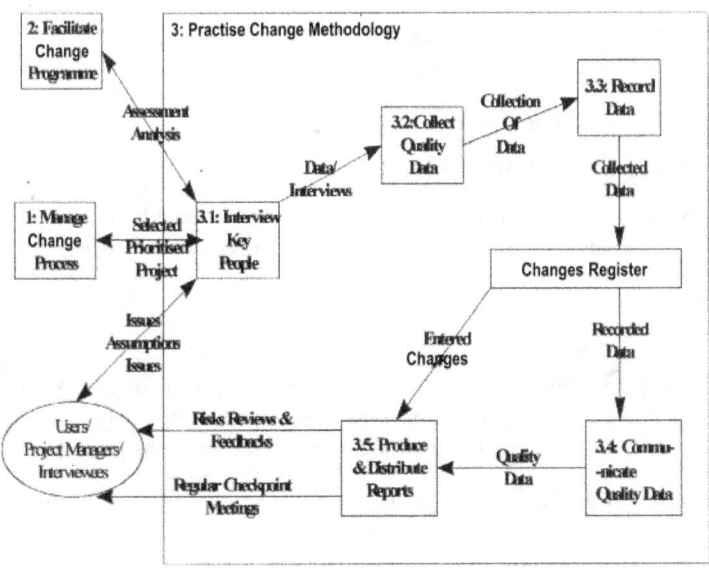

RELATIONSHIP OF DATAFLOW DIAGRAMS

All dataflow diagrams shown in above pages are based on the PsySys Limited manuals and handouts as used for the training.

DATAFLOW DIAGRAMS:	DESCRIPTION OF DIAGRAMS AND THEIR PROCESSES.
0: Manage Change Programme	• Project: something complex that you want (plan) to happen. • Change: Something that you don't want to happen. • Project management: Planning and making things happen. • Change management: Attacking anything that might disturb the plans
1: Manage Change Process	The process consists of an integrated closed loop method which logically progresses through: 1.1 Project Prioritisation, 1.2 Strategic Cost Analysis, 1.3 Assessment Analysis, 1.4 Work Plan Analysis, 1.5 Risk Prioritisation, 1.6 Change Control.
1.1 Prioritise Project	Only complex and critical projects need to have a fully structured Change Management process in place.
1.2 Analyse Strategic Cost	Strategic Cost Analysis provides a means of assessing the cost Change in a project in its very early stages and "kick-starts" the Change Management process.
1.3 Analyse Assessment	Fundamentally, projects only fail due to two reasons either the wrong assumptions were made or the significance of the assumptions was not understood.
1.4 Analyse Work plan	Work Plan Analysis may be used to focus on the risky areas of detailed, multi-level project plans when time is of the essence.

1.5 Prioritise Change	Prioritisation allows the Project Manager to divert limited resources at the most critical project change.
1.6 Control Change	Changes may be attacked at both the strategic and tactical levels. Strategic approaches look for trends and underlying causes for groups of Changes. Tactical approaches take each Change at face value.
2: Facilitate Change Programme	The Change Management Programme is essentially a framework process that allows the capture of collective knowledge and viewpoints from those involved on the project, in a form that facilitates communication of events, assessments and ensures pro-active management of changes. By dramatically improving communication, Changes are avoided, or managed proactively and project objectives are delivered on time.
2.1: Analyse Assessment	The core is Assessment Analysis. This uses structured techniques to analyse project plans and identify the most sensitive assumptions that are potentially unstable, and therefore the source of greatest change.
2.2: Question Event	Events are open questions, which are holding up plans/implementation. An Event is any open question, which has been asked at the right time to which a high quality answer cannot be provided without escalation.
2.3: Raise Assessment	Making Assessments in plans closes many Events. An Assessment is a single, simple, positive or negative statement.
2.4: Manage Changes	Unstable/sensitive assumptions create changes. Significant changes need to be managed formally. Definition: A Change is a simple statement of the form: "IF" Assumption proves incorrect, "THEN" Describe the impact.
2.5: Plan Changes	Change Plans impact project plans. Events, Assessments, and changes are inherent in the

	project plans. Population of assessment and risks registers by progressing Change Plans/Main/Project Plans.
3: Practise Change Methodology	The Role of a Change Management Practitioner includes: • Interview 'Key People' within the project, • To collect 'Quality' data, • Ensure the data collected is recorded in the Change Register, • Communicate the 'Quality' data to Project staff, • Produces accurate and timely reports for meetings: • Weekly Check Point Meetings, • Change Review Boards.
3.1: Interview Key People	Identifying the right people to interview is critical to producing a comprehensive and coherent picture of the changes facing a project. So, to decide who should be interviewed, start with the project or programme organisational structure. Depending on the scope of the change assessment it may be necessary to map the organisational hierarchy to ensure that the right people are interviewed and that the risks arising are reviewed at an appropriate level.
3.2: Collect Quality Data	This function requires to: • Interview 'Key People' within the project, • Collect 'Quality' data.
3.3: Record Data	Having Interviewed the 'Key People' within the project and collected the 'Quality' data: • Ensure the data collected is recorded in the Change Register.
3.4: Communicate Quality Data	The interviews of 'Key People' within the project have been completed, the 'Quality' data recorded in the Change Register and communicated to Project staff, the next function is: • Facilitate and ensure the Change

	Management process stays on track.
3.5: Produce Reports	After the initial round of interviews, a suitable forum must be established to discuss the changes identified.
	The best method is to establish a specific Change Review Meeting with a representation consisting of the Change Owners and chaired by the Programme Director or the process 'champion' in the client organisation.
	The main function is to:
	• Produce accurate and timely reports for meetings,
	• Weekly Check Point Meetings,
	• Change Review Boards.

Database Of Events, Assessments, and Changes Register Description.	
Data Store: *Changes Register*	All events, assessments, and changes captured should be held in a Changes Register.
	Remember, only critical assessments will be converted into changes and held in a Change Register.
	Thus, by filtering the assessments and consolidating them into changes, all information captured will be rationalised and details of their source and consequences will be traceable.

The purpose for this process is for the identification of those assets of the project that need to be made into configuration items, and to control those items throughout the lifecycle. Also, to follow the Configuration Management procedures defined for the project and to ensure the version of each configuration item that applies to the development, test and live environments is known.

Configuration Management ensures that any changes applied to any configuration item are tracked and are auditable. It allows periodic baselines to be drawn where configuration items synchronise and the whole project is in a 'known state'.

The level of formality required, to be applied to configuration management must be commensurate with the size, nature and importance of the project. The approach to configuration management will be documented in the Project Plan and must be in place before major development starts, that is, at the end of Business Study.

RELEASE PROCEDURES

Configuration management has a close relationship with change control and release procedures. If a configuration management tool is used, then ensure that staff is trained in its use. Define which products from each phase are to be placed under configuration management. Involve the release management team as early as possible as they will have an interest in the Configuration Management strategy adopted for the project.

Configuration Management is particularly important throughout development when using an iterative approach. Therefore, how staff will be made aware of the configuration management tools, procedures, etc. when they join the project.

At the end of the Business Study the Prioritised Requirements List, Business Area Definition and System Architecture Definition should all be base-lined. These products will still evolve through the remainder of the project. Keep the Trace ability Matrix from the beginning. If projects are developing iteratively, consider producing a daily software build as a way of base-lining the system and identifying integration problems.

CRITICAL PROJECTS

Consult the Configuration Management Team before and during your project. Use the database under the care of the Configuration Management Team and follow the instructions in the guidelines especially concerning configuration baseline contents and the minimum baseline. Project technical documents may be stored and published.

TANGIBLE FIXED ASSETS

Tangible fixed assets should be valued at the lower of replacement cost and recoverable amount. Recoverable amount is defined as the higher of net realisable value and value in use. This can be expressed diagrammatically. The replacement cost for different classes of assets is described in the following paragraphs.

Impairment occurs where the recoverable amount falls below replacement cost. The replacement cost for operational land and buildings exists use value. In the case of specialised properties or properties not normally traded on the open market, valuation on this basis may be inappropriate and/or impractical and such property should be valued on the basis of depreciated replacement cost.

OPERATIONAL ASSETS

Other (non-property) operational assets should be valued on the basis of depreciated replacement cost. The normal basis of valuation may not be appropriate if a modern substitute is markedly different in its cost, life, or output, or where technological advances have resulted in likely replacements having significantly improved quality or quantity of outputs. Under such circumstances, it will be necessary to undertake an "equivalent asset" calculation to arrive at a replacement cost the asset.

Impairment occurs where the recoverable amount of an asset is lower than its replacement cost.

NON-PROFIT ACTIVITIES

The not-for-profit nature of the vast majority of activities means that value in use is not measurable in terms of income. In these cases, value in use will be assumed to be at least equal to the cost of replacing the service potential provided by the asset, unless there has been a reduction in that service potential.

Such a reduction can arise for various reasons, including:

- The purpose for which the asset was acquired is no longer carried;
- Out and there is no alternative use for the asset;
- The asset is to be sold;
- The asset cannot be used;
- The asset is otherwise surplus and has no alternative use;
- The asset is over-specified for its current use.

The recoverable amount will be the asset's net realisable value, i.e. the amount at which the asset could be disposed of, less any disposal costs.

Consideration should also be given to the residual value of assets created during the project, at the end of the appraisal period.

DISPOSAL OF ASSETS

Disposal of assets, especially high value assets and property, needs to be conducted with the same scrupulous rigour as the acquisition of those assets. For major assets, the process of disposal follows the stages where decisions about investment are made in the context of achieving an appropriate return for the release of the asset.

RELEASE

The purpose for this activity is to group all the individual products of the project (code, training docs, new business procedures etc) together into a coherent configured whole. The ultimate purpose for this is to perform the final test on the configured release.

Testing must be integrated throughout the lifecycle. This is not the first time the whole system has been system tested. As long the previous testing has been integrated properly this final test should be very quick and not find many additional bugs.

The final test must address all elements of the product. This will include code, installation procedures, and training documents, changed business procedures.

The process to be used for release will differ, depending on the type of application being delivered by the project. For example: Electronic Self Service programme have defined a process suitable for their applications.

RELEASE PLANS

The release plans should provide the ability to indicate where a particular requirement has been designed, built and tested. The Project Configuration Management Plan (sub-product of Project Plan) should document the approach the project will take to manage the project's assets.

As such the following activities should be included:

• Identify the roles to be involved in performing configuration management;

• Identify any tools that may be used to facilitate the management procedures;

• Describe the procedures that will be used to perform configuration and change management.

DOCUMENTATION

Project documentation that satisfies the Change Management process must be included and identified. Definitive documents must be visible to the project and Reviewers. If it is to be a model for others it must be visible programme wide and all documentation must be under version control. All changes must be documented and there must be a register of published documents.

Project Software Repository Source code should be readable by only those who need to know and such software should be subject to an audit trail of who has, who amended etc. All software should be uniquely identifiable and versioned.

The level of formality required, to be applied to configuration management must be commensurate with the size, nature and importance of the project. The approach to configuration management will be documented in the Project Plan and must be in place before major development starts, that is, at the end of Business Study. Configuration management has a close relationship with change control and release procedures. If a configuration management tool is used then ensure that staff is trained in its use.

DEFINITION OF PRODUCTS

Define which products from each phase are to be placed in configuration management. Involve the release management team as early as possible as they will have an interest in the Configuration Management strategy adopted for the project.

PROCUREMENT

'Procurement' means the whole process of acquisition from third parties (including the logistical aspects) and covers goods, services and construction projects. This process spans the whole life cycle from initial concept and definition of business needs through to the end of the useful life of an asset or end of a services contract. Both conventionally funded and more innovative types of funded projects are included. The process is not limited to the purchasing function in organisations and is inherently multi-functional especially in large, complex procurements.

REVIEWS

Any Process will define review points throughout the lifecycle of acquisition projects. Reviews are undertaken for procurement projects of all levels of change. Requests for Reviews are initiated by Senior Responsible Owners.

Additional interim Reviews may sometimes be carried out during the life of a procurement project. For a big project that has a long time span between Reviews, an additional Review may be arranged before a significant decision point e.g. the announcement of a preferred supplier). Additional reviews may also be beneficial where added assurance is needed or where there are specific areas of concern. These reviews are often referred to as Peer Reviews.

A Review is held before key decision points in the lifecycle of a procurement project. The review teams are made up of independent experienced practitioners who bring their prior knowledge and skills to bear to identify the key issues that need to be addressed for the project to succeed. The review criteria are established and published in a set of workbooks available on an intranet and website. The work of a Review team is for the project, and ownership of the review report and recommendations lies with this team.

A Review is carried out over a period of 4-5 days at the most with the review report presented and discussed with the team before the review team leaves the client premises.

AUDIT

Internal Audit primarily provides an independent and objective opinion to the Accounting Officer on change management, control and governance, by measuring and evaluating their effectiveness in achieving an organisation's agreed objectives. In most organisational bodies Internal Audit reports go directly to the Accounting Officer (Chief Executive). In order for Internal Audit to provide the Accounting Officer with an objective opinion, the Chief Executive and the Audit Committee develop an audit strategy in consultation with, and subject to approval.

The audit plan is circulated to senior members of the organisation and advance notice will be given prior to the commencement of a review. Under normal circumstances Terms of Reference will be produced for each audit assignment and these will be discussed and agreed with management. The views and opinions of management will be obtained at the end of each review and the final report will contain an agreed action plan, which will contain the name of the of the officer responsible for each recommendation and a target date for full implementation.

REVIEW PROCESS

In short, to secure the release of dual key monies, it has to be demonstrated that:

1. The programme is aligned with the strategy,

2. They are implementing the recommendations in the report for the projects within each programme,

3. They have plans in place to realise the benefits of the investment.

Much of the evidence needed to meet these criteria is capable of being derived from two complementary processes:

1. The development of business strategies,

2. The various Reviews.

The Change Management process is designed as an aid to companies rather than as an external audit of projects.

DIFFERENCE OF PROGRAMME AND PROJECT

A project is a particular way of managing activities to deliver specific products over a specified period of time and within defined cost and resource constraints. A programme is a management framework for co-ordinating related projects and work-streams to deliver strategic outcomes and benefits over timescales that are often less well defined.

A strategic assessment is designed to apply at the start of an acquisition programme and may be repeated at subsequent key decision points. A Review can confirm that the appropriate project structure is in place and that interdependencies have been recognised.

Reviews apply to each of the procurement projects within the programme. A repeat Review later in the life of a programme can be helpful to re-visit and confirm the business case, the management of the programme changes and interactions between the projects and the delivery of benefits for the programme as a whole.

Financial value is only one of the factors to consider when deciding on the level of change faced by a programme or project. This is recognised within the Change Assessment. The fact that a programme or project environment has been deemed appropriate indicates that there is uniqueness to the programme or project, which, in turn, indicates a level of inherent change. For example, the programme or project could be of low cost but, if unsuccessful, could have a major impact upon staff morale within an organisation. Reviews are scaleable. Acquisition programmes and procurement projects should, therefore, receive a level of Review appropriate to the level of change associated.

Organisations should use Change Management and Assessment to determine the change level of their programmes and projects and to understand the nature of the changes associated with them in a structured and systematic way. Programmes or projects classified as needing small change are likely to contain significant procurements.

In certain cases, a Process was originally set up to help procurement projects that involve external (actual) expenditure. However, even on projects being "developed in house", there would normally be additional expenditure on hardware, software, licensing, increased network capacity, consultancy support. The change analysis would, of course, indicate whether to involve further reviews or whether it is small change and carried out by in house staff (and of course it is arguable that "in house developments/solutions" are smaller changes given that the client has to retain financial, technical and managerial changes compared to outsourced deals).

To summarise, technically non-procurement activities are out of the scope, but this takes a very narrow view of the benefits that can arise from a review (assurance that the project likely to be successful or, if not, remedial actions proposed).

Pilot procurement projects have the same characteristics as other procurement projects. The fact that a pilot is being managed within a project structure itself indicates that there is a unique environment, which, in turn, indicates a level of inherent risk. An assessment review should be completed in the usual way to determine the risk associated with the project.

Projects utilising existing contractual arrangements will still benefit from the added value provided by the process of reviewing and assessing, in that the majority of the issues addressed will still apply. In these cases Reviews may be scaled down where the procurement strategy is largely predetermined and standard procedures exist for the take on of new work packages.

As usual reviews start up operability and the results achieved and lessons learnt. There is evidence that anything less than a well disciplined use of framework contracts with sound management processes akin to any project leads these contracts to becoming a leaky sieve for companies and a source of high margins to suppliers. With the growth of framework arrangements it is mandatory for such call offs in central civil government and international organisations to be exposed to the appropriate level of Reviews.

A successful company would provide sufficient staff to the pool to cover the resourcing of procurement reviews. Staff will need to be trained and accredited as reviewers. You need to assign a coordinator to administer the reviews, the process roll out of changes within projects, the staff provision and the communications and training programme in house. Changes are undertaken by the Review Team Leader and nominated members.

The Project Manager should arrange an initial assessment meeting. The purpose of the assessment meeting is to agree the change level of the project (low, medium or high), to enable those responsible for the individual changes to gain an understanding of the programme/project and to establish readiness for solutions to the problems.

Notice is required following the assessment meeting in order to assemble a review team and hold the necessary prior Planning Meeting. The revised assessment may indicate a change to the change level associated with the programme or project and therefore a change to subsequent handling within the process. In that eventuality the team will discuss the way forward.

The Review Planning Meeting has, following senior staff support, been established as essential to the delivery of reviews of changes I the various projects. It is designed as a facilitated workshop at which the Senior Responsible Owner, review team and project team jointly plan their approach to the review. The planning meeting is envisaged as a mandatory part of all new reviews of changes.

The value of these planning meetings is such that only (as an example) the Programmes Director/Manager for the project/s has the authority to modify this policy. The Programmes Director/Manager may recommend earliest and continued intervention to increase the likelihood of success. The team/s involved will then agree an overall traffic light assessment for inclusion in the report at the end of each review.

TRAFFIC LIGHTS

The definitions of the 'traffic lights' are:

Red – To achieve success the programme or project should take remedial action immediately. It means 'fix the changes/key problems fast', not 'stop the project'.

Amber – The programme or project should go forward with actions on recommendations to be carried out before the next review.

Green – the programme or project is on target to succeed but may benefit from the uptake of the recommendations.

Reports and reviews should be conducted on a confidential basis. This approach promotes an open and honest exchange between the programme/project and review teams delivering maximum added value. Responsibility for the quality of the workshop and ownership of the materials used will remain with Programmes Director/Manager.

An interim review can be conducted between two major reviews, where there are interim decision points e.g. one at preferred bidder stage and the other at best and final offers. For property/construction projects, the interim reviews could be at outline design and detailed design.

MANAGING REQUIREMENTS CHANGES

This briefing looks at an issue that is fundamental to the success of any commercial relationship that is to succeed over time, the ability to accommodate change successfully. Managing the change at the end of the requirements contract is perhaps the biggest challenge of all.

Changes to requirements can be small adjustments to existing service specifications, planned modular/incremental developments, major business change leading to completely new services - or anything in between. In the context of this briefing, changes are significant enough to require management involvement.

The need to negotiate change is a continuing and ongoing component of service contracts. The ability to accommodate change successfully is fundamental to the success of any commercial arrangement that is to succeed over time; partnerships are increasingly seen as a way of coping with uncertainty, as their purpose is to accommodate change effectively and efficiently. The need to negotiate change is a continuing and on-going component of partnerships. It may be an important issue too in more conventional contractual arrangements.

PARTNERSHIP ARRANGEMENT

This briefing assumes a partnership arrangement, but the principles apply generally. Maintenance of existing systems involves ongoing changes to requirements. It is a major cost that requires careful attention.

Business managers and service providers are responsible for identifying the need for change in response to user demand or changes in the business. Service providers manage the implementation and provision of new or updated services. There may be an informed customer role providing the interface between the customer and provider. In addition, there may be programme/project teams who are involved in modular or incremental change.

REQUIREMENTS FOR CHANGE

The requirements/drivers for change during the term of the requirements contract can derive from a range of internal or external sources.

Internal change could include:

- Evolving business requirements,
- Changes in the customer's roles/responsibilities,
- Statutory developments,
- Boundary of responsibility changes,
- Rationalisation of roles,
- New developments,
- Provider restructuring, merger or acquisition,
- Revised management, reporting and/or approvals chains,
- Significant revisions to the corporate strategy/business,
- External sources of change, such as developments in technology,
- Economic trends which affect the profitability/value for money,
- The need to provide electronic forms of service delivery,
- Meet customer expectation.

CHANGE CONTROL PROCEDURE

A single change control procedure should apply to all changes, although there may be certain delegated or shortened procedures available in defined circumstances – such as delegated budget tolerance levels within which a manager would not have to seek senior management approval. However, flexibility needs to be built into this procedure to deal with issues such as emergencies.

A change control procedure should provide a clear set of steps and clearly allocated responsibilities covering:

- Requesting changes,
- Assessment of impact,
- Prioritisation and authorisation,
- Agreement with provider,
- Control of implementation,
- Documentation of change assessments and orders.

AUTHORISATION

Responsibility for authorising different types of change will often rest with different people, and documented internal procedures will need to reflect this. In particular, changes to the overall contract, such as changes to prices outside the scope of agreed price variation mechanisms must have senior management approval.

In many cases it will be possible to delegate limited powers to authorise minor changes, which affect particular services or Service Level Agreements using agreed processes.

Change during the term of a contract can be categorised as follows:

- Planned/routine change,
- Proactive change programmes,
- Unplanned change.

PLANNED CHANGE

This could include modular and incremental developments, such as planning for changes to user requirements, refurbishment of workspace, maintenance/enhancements to existing systems or planned technology refreshment. This type of change is most easily accommodated under, and is best suited to, formal change management processes.

Well-constructed contractual agreements should express provisions detailing the procedures to be adopted in initiating, discussing and delivering change through:

- User groups,
- Change control boards,
- Formal approvals processes,

- Benefits management regimes.

The procedures to be adopted for the escalation and resolution of disputes that may arise, such as:

- Defined escalation routes and timescales,

- Alternative dispute resolution procedures (neutral advisors, expert determination, arbitration),

The procedure for making amendments to the contract documentation:

- QA procedures (including legal QA),

- Authorisations (individual authorised signing powers)

- Audit trail.

PRO-ACTIVE CHANGE PROGRAMMES

Change need not necessarily always be reactive in nature. It can be initiated deliberately as a proactive approach. There could, for example, be an element of business transformation to drive forward a change programme. In this way the contract is used as a vehicle to deliver efficiency improvements and associated cost savings from the re-engineering of the customer's internal business processes, facilitated by the use of technology.

The details of approaches taken in each project to date have been different, but a typical partnership arrangement might be (in summary):

- Step 1: provider proposes business change project to customer,

- Step 2: customer approves project on basis of agreed cost/benefit model,

- Step 3: provider develops and implements new service to support new business process (at provider's risk),

- Step 4: implement and adopt new business processes,

- Step 5: both parties measure resultant cost savings to customer using agreed cost/benefit model,

- Step 6: provider's service charges calculated as a percentage of realised cost savings to customer.

Recent contracts show an emerging trend. Over the life of partnership as a whole, the expectation of the parties, sometimes underwritten by contractual guarantees from the provider, is that the aggregate cost savings to the customer over the term of the partnership may in fact exceed the aggregate 'core' service payable by the customer. The viability/appropriateness of approach outlined above of course depends on the nature of the partnership, the customer organisation (in terms of its receptiveness to change, potential for improvement in existing business processes etc), and the services to be delivered.

UNPLANNED CHANGE

Unplanned change is imposed on the partnership from outside (for example, resulting from a change in some aspect of the external environment). This is the most difficult type of change to manage and accommodate. It is also potentially the most damaging to the partnership. It can hit the partnership unannounced and require immediate action by both parties. At worst it can serve to invalidate the deal for one or both parties, resulting in unplanned conclusion of the programme or even the partnership.

Unplanned change will test the strength of the partnership relationship, and the capabilities of its management. The response to un-planned change is crucial and must be structured. In response to unplanned change, the partnership (that is both parties in co-operation), must undertake the following analysis:

• Step 1: understand and assess the impact of the change on partnership. Can this be dealt with under the existing change management procedures or does this require specialised management?

• Step 2: escalate within both partner organisations as appropriate,

• Step 3: review the basis of the deal – does the original deal remain viable for both parties?

• Step 4: assess the extent of change required to the deal,

• Step 5: negotiate the required amendments.

From the customer's perspective as the public sector partner a key decision point is often reached at Step 4 above. It may be necessary for both partners to make real, and sometimes significant, concessions in the resulting negotiations in order to make the deal work for the future. A complete audit trail of developments is essential to ensure public accountability, but you must be prepared to make bold judgments where necessary to ensure the survival of the partnership (subject to the overall deal remaining viable to the public sector partner). Your decision-making must be driven by clear business objectives of the organisation.

MAIN CHANGE MANAGEMENT POINTS

A change is an uncertain event, which may have an adverse effect on the project's objectives. Using Change Management should be very effective in the quest for identifying changes throughout the project lifecycle.

Remember, Change Management is:

- Forward looking, investigating problems and how to deal with threats,

- A tool enabling communication, getting people at all levels to talk to each other and to interact,

- A no blame team culture, bringing concerns into the open where actions can be taken and plans put in place, in order to stop a change occurring.

IDENTIFICATION OF RISKY PROJECTS

The Change Management process commences by identifying the enterprises most important and risky projects, as these must be given priority. Change Management is essentially a method that permits the collection of knowledge and experience from those involved, in a form that facilitates the Systematic Interaction and Generic Methodology for Applications:

SYSTEMATIC

The varied events, their assessments, and the consequential risks relating to or consisting of a system. Methodical in procedures and plans, these are addressed to those involved and deliberating within the parameters of their systems development responsibilities. The results will depend on interaction.

INTERACTION

The mutual or reciprocal action which encourages those involved in the programmes and projects to communicate with each other and to work closely with a view to solving the threatening events before they impact on the development of the system. The individuals involved maintain a generic approach.

GENERIC APPROACH

Relates and characterises the whole group of those involved in assessing the events and attacking the threatening ones, before they become risks to the development of the system. The end result being the avoidance of apparent problems, within the pre-defined users systems requirements. This is enabled by following the establish methodology.

METHODOLOGY

The system architects and the change management practitioners

simply follow the approved body of systems development methods,

rules and management procedures employed by their organisation. For

practical or even ethical reasons, it must be noted that with such a

philosophy, it is seldom possible to fulfil all requirements of very large

organisational systems. As such, the Change Management

methodology ought to be obligatory and as such it should be

administered in all applications.

APPLICATIONS

Putting to use such techniques and in applying the change management principles in the development of various applications will involve numerous and varied activities. A concrete issue in developing new applications is the problem of communication among the people involved, the motivation constantly needed for generic work, the ability to interact systematically and in using a structured systems methodology.

CONFIGURATION, RELEASE, ASSETS

Change Management and the changes to Configuration, Release, and Assets as a whole group of activities have traditionally been concerned with finding effective solutions to specific operational problems. The purpose of this book is to look at current problems and new, better methods, techniques, and tools for processing changes. In the past, it has been found that too many of the solutions are not implemented and, of those that are, too few survive the inclination of client functional areas to return to familiar ways of doing things. Therefore, Change Management personnel have gradually come to realise that their tasks should not only include solving specific problems but also designing problem-solving and implementation systems that predict and prevent future problems, identify and solve current ones, and implement and maintain these solutions under changing conditions.

COMPONENTS OF CHANGES

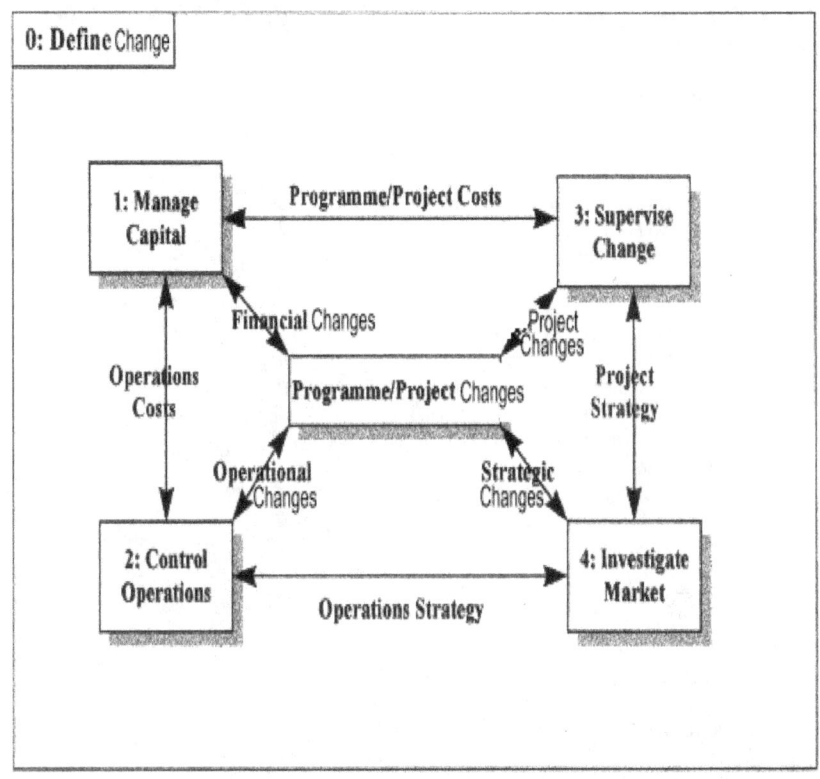

The Components Of The Total Business Changes

INDEX OF CHAPTERS: PAGE:

BIBLIOGRAPHY:

A Sofroniou, The Management Of Commercial Computing, PsySys Limited, ISBN: 0 9527956 0 4.

A Sofroniou, Structured Management Techniques, Association For Psychological Counselling And Training, Training Material, 1984.

A Sofroniou, Structured Systems Methodologies, Published and unpublished lecture notes, 1987 -1997.

A Sofroniou, Management Styles lectures, 1982.

A Sofroniou, Thesis submission on Automotive Components and Materials Purchasing System for Engineering Qualifications, 1983.

A Sofroniou, Collaborative project on Knowledge-base, Expert Systems and Artificial Intelligence, with Imperial College, Logica plc and The Engineering Industry Training Board, 1985-1986.

A Sofroniou, Rapid Structured Methodology for Life Assurance Systems, 1990-1992.

A Sofroniou, Analysis and Design project on EPoS Retail and Logistic System, 1995.

A Sofroniou, Research project, a study on COTS (Commercial Off The Shelf) Packages, 1995.

A Sofroniou, Technical Design projects for Internet Integration, Security, Client/Servers, Data Warehousing and Databases, 1996-1997.

A Sofroniou, The Year 2000 Project and Planning Procedures for European Group of Companies, 1998.

Ian Graham, Object Oriented Methods, Addison Wesley, ISBN: 0 201 56521 8.

E Yourdon and L Constantine, Structured Design, Yourdon inc., 1975.

Chris Gane and Trish Sarson, Structured Systems Analysis: Tools and Techniques, Improved System Technologies, Inc., 1977.